THE PSYCHOLOGY OF DIETING

Why do some of us become overweight? Why is it so difficult to lose weight? How can we adopt healthy attitudes towards food?

The Psychology of Dieting takes a broad and balanced view of the causes of weight gain and the challenges involved in dieting. Exploring the cognitive, emotional and social triggers which lead us to make poor decisions around food, the book considers what it means to diet well. By understanding our psychological selves, the book shows how we can change our unhealthy behaviours and potentially lose weight.

In an era of weight problems, obesity and dangerous dieting, The Psychology of Dieting shows us that there is no such thing as a miracle diet, and that we must understand how our minds shape the food choices we make.

Jane Ogden is Professor of Health Psychology at the University of Surrey, UK. She has been involved in research and writing about eating behaviour and weight management for nearly 30 years and is a frequent contributor to the media for magazines, radio and TV.

THE PSYCHOLOGY OF EVERYTHING

The Psychology of Everything is a series of books which debunk the myths and pseudo-science surrounding some of life's biggest questions.

The series explores the hidden psychological factors that drive us, from our sub-conscious desires and aversions, to the innate social instincts handed to us across the generations. Accessible, informative, and always intriguing, each book is written by an expert in the field, examining how research-based knowledge compares with popular wisdom, and illustrating the potential of psychology to enrich our understanding of humanity and modern life.

Applying a psychological lens to an array of topics and contemporary concerns – from sex to addiction to conspiracy theories – The Psychology of Everything will make you look at everything in a new way.

Titles in the series:

For further information about this series please visit
www.thepsychologyofeverything.co.uk

THE PSYCHOLOGY OF DIETING

JANE OGDEN

Routledge
Taylor & Francis Group

LONDON AND NEW YORK

First published 2018
by Routledge
2 Park Square, Milton Park, Abingdon, Oxon OX14 4RN

and by Routledge
605 Third Avenue, New York, NY 10017

Routledge is an imprint of the Taylor & Francis Group, an informa business

© 2018 Jane Ogden

British Library Cataloguing-in-Publication Data
A catalogue record for this book is available from the British Library

Library of Congress Cataloging-in-Publication Data
A catalog record for this book has been requested

ISBN: 978-1-138-50121-8 (hbk)
ISBN: 978-1-138-50125-6 (pbk)
ISBN: 978-1-315-14422-1 (ebk)

Typeset in Joanna
by Apex CoVantage, LLC

CONTENTS

PREFACE

THE AIM OF THIS BOOK

There are many, many books on dieting on the market. The vast majority are diet books which are characterised by a clear, simple message targeting those who want to lose weight that is not grounded in any evidence. These make weight loss look easy, massively overstate the likelihood of weight loss maintenance and as a result sell loads! There are also more balanced books which explore the complexities of eating behaviour, weight loss, eating disorders and obesity, but these are either edited volumes for health professionals or authored books such as my own *The Psychology of Eating* which are heavily referenced and aimed at students looking for academic support for their own research. *The Psychology of Dieting* aims to present an accessible and concise account of the issues surrounding dieting which is easy to read but still grounded in evidence. It explores the history of dieting, why people diet, the positive and negative consequences of dieting and the reasons why dieting either succeeds or fails. It then explores possible strategies for behaviour change and illustrates how these can be used to maximise the success of dieting by encouraging dieting well in a way that can persist for the longer term. *The Psychology of Dieting* does not have a magic pill for weight loss success (sorry!).

But it does offer a series of evidence-based strategies and suggestions to try (and try again) that should maximise the chance of success in the end. There is the phrase 'you can't please all of the people all of the time'. I believe that no one approach to dieting can work for all of the people all of the time. But in *The Psychology of Dieting* I hope that there are enough possible approaches for most of the people to find something (or even many things) that works for them or for those they want to help.

WHO IS IT FOR?

The Psychology of Dieting is aimed at anyone who needs to lose weight and wants to keep it off but is concerned with being better informed and aware that dieting is not as easy as it is sometimes made out to be. It is also for those who want to help others lose weight, such as slimming club leaders, dieticians, nutritionists, counsellors, psychologists, nurses, personal trainers, partners or parents, and who want to understand the reasons when and why diets succeed or fail and how to encourage others to lose weight in a way that can be sustained into the future.

WHO IS THE AUTHOR?

I am a Professor in Health Psychology at the University of Surrey where I teach psychology, dietician, nutrition and vet students about health psychology in general and specifically about the role of psychological factors in eating behaviour and weight management. I am author of six books, including three on eating behaviour: *Fat Chance: The Myth of Dieting*, *The Psychology of Eating* and *The Good Parenting Food Guide*. I have also published over 180 academic papers, of which about 100 are on aspects of diet, obesity and eating disorders. I am passionate about bringing research and theory to the general public and am a regular contributor to radio and TV, have a column called 'Food Fights' for *The Conversation* and have written articles for newspapers and magazines.

HOW TO READ THIS BOOK

Obviously I can't dictate how readers choose to use this book! But I have given it to health professionals and dieters to read and they have all commented how much they like the way it builds and tells a story. This was my aim! Therefore I would strongly recommend that you start at the beginning and make your way through to the end. But to help you, the story is: we overeat because of what's in our heads and triggers in the environment. To eat less we need to change what's in our head and manage the environment. Here's how to do it! But – still read it all the way through. It's very short after all!

1

A BRIEF HISTORY OF DIETING

For as long as there have been artefacts to discover, records kept and images drawn, women and men have wanted to change how they look. Cave paintings show body adornments and painted faces, ancient digs discover combs and jewellery and Egyptian tombs were packed full of elaborate masks and clothing. More recently women have turned to corsets and lacing, bras and rubber roll-ons, and men either grew facial hair or immaculately shaved at least some of it off. But the body remained something to be modified in line with current trends and fashions.

And then in the 20th century dieting emerged, along with the need to transform the body in a more permanent way. This can be seen through the media and fashion industry, the changing shape of the ideal body and the rise of the dieting industry. It can also be seen in the backlash against dieting that emerged in the 1980s and the current state of play with a proliferation of dieting books and classes. This chapter will explore this history of dieting to illustrate the need for an evidence-based approach – the notion of dieting well.

THE MEDIA AND FASHION INDUSTRY

For centuries, whalebones, latex, nylon and cotton have been used to reshape and rearrange any aspect of the body which did not conform.

Think Jane Austen's Elizabeth Bennett in the 1800s with her Empire line dresses to show off her ample bosom, the painfully tight corsets worn by Flaubert's Madam Bovary in the 1820s, causing her to forever faint, and the hooped skirts in the 1850s emphasising a narrow waist and larger bottom. Even in the 'flapper' days of the 1920s, bras and corsets were an acceptable way to bind down breasts and flatten stomachs.

Then in the late 1960s, women traded in wired and laced corsets for the rubber variety, which in turn were traded in for freedom. Boadicea-like bras were exchanged for the softer, lighter versions which were in turn exchanged for the luxury of going braless. Women were allowed and even expected to release their bodies and to resort to the natural support of flesh and muscles. And then there came the bikini, and along with it Twiggy was launched enthusiastically onto the fashion scene. Suddenly at the beginning of an era of natural control and natural support, women were told that they should not have any flesh to control or support. Bikinis gave no protection and represented a freedom that was only available to those without any excess bodily fat. Twiggy did not need to wear a bra or corset; she had no need to squash her body in, only for it to reappear elsewhere. But this absence of need came not from a desire to free the female body but from the very fact that she had nothing to free. Women could go braless as long as their breasts revealed only a restrained life of their own, and corsets were out as long as what was left behind did not need a corset. And this is where dieting raised its head. Long before the onset of the obesity epidemic, the '60s represented the onset of the dieting boom, and central to this boom was the dieting industry, which has been on the increase ever since.

THE DIETING INDUSTRY

Books, magazines, dieting clubs, newspaper articles, TV programmes, dieting aids, apps, online support groups and exercise videos all make up the dieting industry. This industry has provided a resource for those who need to lose weight. But it has also changed the way in which we think about body size in terms of the stereotypes we hold and a sense that body size can be changed.

Providing a resource

Weight Watchers started in America in 1963 and in Britain in 1967, and the first copy of *Slimming* magazine was issued in Britain in 1969. *Slimmer* sold 142,000 copies between January and June in 1990; Weight Watchers UK had an average of 140,000 members, and Slimmer clubs had an average of 40,000 members. Wolf (1990) described the $33 billion a year diet industry in the US, Eyton's *The F Plan Diet* (1982) sold 810,000 copies in three weeks and *Rosemary Conley's Complete Hip and Thigh Diet* (1989) has sold over 2 million copies. GP services now also offer support for weight loss and the NHS has services for weight loss at various centres around the UK. There is a need for these services, as people respond to their availability. The dieting industry therefore provides a resource for its users by offering information in leaflets, books, face to face contact or on websites, by providing opportunities for networking and group support and by delivering expert care through weigh-ins and reinforcement. This is all useful. But the dieting industry also changes the way we think about body size.

Stereotypes about size

There are many stereotypes associated with body size, and whilst thinness is mostly associated with attractiveness, a sense of control and emotional stability, overweight is associated with being unattractive, being out of control, lacking willpower and laziness. These ideas come from the media and fashion industry. They are also perpetuated by the diet industry that uses slim models to sell the latest low-calorie ready meals, meal replacements, chocolate bars and over-the-counter drugs and model the latest clothes. Often the emphasis is simply on becoming more attractive through losing weight. For example, Mazel in her *Beverly Hills Diet* (1981) suggested that if someone should comment, 'You're getting too thin', you should reply, 'Thank you'[1].

Likewise, magazines publish success stories of women who have lost weight which illustrate how much happier these women feel and how their lives have changed. As Twigg (1997) says of his 'Kensington diet', it can "achieve a huge amount for you, including making you look and feel healthier, happier, younger and more zestful"[2] (p. 20).

Sometimes the emphasis is control. For example, Conley, who developed the *Complete Hip and Thigh Diet* (1989) and others such as the *Complete Flat Stomach Plan* (1996) and *Metabolism Booster Diet* (1991), wrote that overweight people must have eaten 'too many fatty and sugary foods which are positively loaded with calories – bread spread with lashings of butter, an abundance of fried foods, cream cakes, biscuits, chocolates, crisps and so on. The types of foods overweight people love'[3] (p. 65). Similarly, in *The Beverly Hills Diet* (1981), Mazel wrote, 'It is imperative that you exercise control when you eat combinations. Don't let your heart take over. Eat like a human being, not a fat person'.

And sometimes the diet industry simply associates being overweight with some deep-rooted psychological problems. For example, Levine (1997), in her book *I Wish I Were Thin, I Wish I Were Fat*, argued that women unconsciously want to be fat and that this is why they overeat; if they can come to terms with these unconscious desires, they can 'finally fulfill our conscious wish to be thin'[4] (p. 13). In fact, Conley (1996) described one woman who lost weight using her diet but regained it and stated that 'Vivien has had a few personal problems and has regained some of her weight. However, she has resolved to try and lose it again as she was so delighted with her previous success'[5] (p. 30). The dieting industry changed the way we think about body size and encouraged us to think that thinness was attractive whilst being overweight was a sign of poor control and psychological problems. Further, this powerful industry also convinced us that body size could be changed and this change was easy as long as we followed their instructions.

Body size can be changed (easily)

Losing weight (and keeping it off) is notoriously hard to do, which is why I am writing this book in order to try to make dieting as effective as it can be! Yet much of the dieting industry presents their product as an inevitable pathway to success. For example, Coleman (1990) opened his book *Eat Green – Lose Weight* with the statement 'You should buy this book if you would like to get slim – and stay slim – and you are fed up with short term diets which either fail or become boring', and later on claimed 'within months you will feel healthier, fitter, stronger and happier'[6] (p. 7). Likewise, De Vries (1989) indicated that his reader should 'make up your mind that this time you will succeed. No more yo-yoing up and down. You're going to lose weight and you are going to lose it permanently'[7] (p. 20), and Twigg (1997), after describing the success of his clients said, 'And if it works for them then I promise you – we're going to make it work for you, too!'[2] (p. 17). Even those diets designed not to reduce fat are described as leading to successful weight loss. For example, Lazarides (1999) described fluid as the root of many people's problems, and said that 'to be able to sit on the loo and urinate away up to 20 lbs of excess body weight in a few days probably sounds like something out of our wildest dreams' but if you stick to her diet 'you will literally be able to urinate much of your excess body weight, sometimes within just a few days'[8] (p. 6). The dieting industry offers its vast range of products as being able to change body weight. It emphasises the success of its products and by doing so reinforces the belief that body size and shape can be easily modified and changed by the individual.

The diet industry has therefore proliferated since the 1960s. But, towards the end of the 20th century the tide started to turn and a backlash to dieting appeared.

THE BACKLASH AGAINST DIETING

Susie Orbach's book *Fat Is a Feminist Issue* was first published in 1978 and highlighted the social pressures to be thin and the complex reasons why women overeat. It was subtitled 'the anti-diet guide'. In 1982, Katahn subtitled his book *How to Stop Dieting Forever*, and his opening statement read, 'I am writing this book because, frankly I am sick and tired of the nonsense being written that offers dieting as a means for permanent weight control'[9] (p. 9). Likewise, the books *Dieting Makes You Fat* by Cannon and Einzig and *Breaking the Diet Habit* by Polivy and Herman were published in 1983. But it was not until the 1990s that the backlash gained momentum, and organisations such as Diet Breakers and the Fat Acceptance movement were set up, books praising the joys of being overweight were written and magazines published articles about 'alternatives to dieting'. For example, Smith (1993) offered her book *Fibrenetics* as a way to 'finally kick the whole concept of dieting out of the window'[10] (p. 12), I published my own book in 1992 called *Fat Chance: The Myth of Dieting Explained* and programmes to encourage 'undieting' were established by researchers such as Janet Polivy and Peter Herman. Particularly in the US, Canada and UK, people became sceptical about the value of dieting, and 'to be on a diet' became tainted with a sense of conformity. This did not, however, stop women dieting. And the shelves were still full of guides to weight loss.

A MORE BALANCED APPROACH

Whilst many fad diets emerge each year and dieters still crave the simple magic pill that will offer them the effortless and successful diet, the past few decades have seen a more balanced approach to dieting. The obesity epidemic took off in the 1980s and in response to this, together with a recognition that dieting is hard, nutritionists, dieticians, psychologists, weight management groups and behaviour change experts now mostly speak of 'healthy eating' or a 'healthy lifestyle' that is sustainable over the longer term. And although this may require the initial impetus of large amounts of weight loss provided by medication, very-low-calorie diets or even surgery, it is increasingly recognised that habits need to change in a way that people can maintain for the rest of their lives. But although the will is now there to do the right thing, it remains unclear what this right thing is. I teach dieticians and nutritionists who are experts in biochemistry and know exactly what people should eat but are crying out for skills on how to get them to change their behaviour. And I meet overweight people who want to lose weight the right way, for the rest of their lives, but are confused by the multitude of messages they receive.

But this isn't to pretend that there is one simple right way to diet, lose weight and keep it off forever. There isn't. There are many different approaches that work for some of the people some of the time. And the aim of this book is to present these approaches to weight loss in an accessible way so that they can be used either by those who need to lose weight or those who want to help others to do the same. I am calling this 'a tool kit for dieting well' and it is the result of 30 years of research and 30 years of refusing to answer the question 'How do I lose weight?' Well, at last I feel as if I might have some sort of answer.

A TOOL KIT FOR DIETING WELL

Being overweight is essentially a product of two factors: what goes on in our heads and the triggers in the environment we live in. These in turn lead to doing less than we should and eating more than we need. The rest of this book will first explore the ways in which these factors promote weight gain, then describe a number of strategies to help people to change what happens in their head as well as manage their environment.

2

BEING OVERWEIGHT OR OBESE

The main reason for dieting is being overweight or obese, and it would have been impossible to miss the epidemic of weight gain that has occurred since about the 1980s. This chapter will describe how to determine if you are overweight and the prevalence, consequences and causes of weight gain in terms of genetics and the environment. The role of behaviour in terms of eating too much and doing too little is key to both weight gain and dieting, and these are covered in the next two chapters (Chapters 3 and 4).

WHAT IS OVERWEIGHT?

Whether or not a person is overweight or obese can be determined using a number of techniques such as waist circumference, percentage of body fat or population norms. But the easiest way is to calculate body mass index (BMI), a ratio between height and weight which can be calculated using any online BMI calculator. This produces a number as follows: normal weight: 18–24.9; overweight: 25–29.9; obese: 30+. Many people who are normal weight diet to change the way they look. This can create a number of problems including body dissatisfaction, eating disorders and even weight gain (see Chapter 5). But many who are overweight or obese also diet to improve their health. This can also create all the same problems as with normal weight people (see Chapter 5). But at times it can also lead to weight loss and improvements in health and well-being. These are the people who should be dieting as long as they diet well.

WHO IS OVERWEIGHT?

Since the 1980s adults have become heavier in most countries of the world. The rates of adult obesity in the UK increased dramatically from 1993 to about 2007 but have been relatively stable for the past few years (11). If obesity is defined as a BMI greater than 30, reports show that in the UK in 1980, 6% of men and 8% of women were obese and that this had increased to 13% and 16% respectively in 1994 and to 22% and 24% in 2009. In 2009 the average BMI was 27 for both men and women. Estimates for the US suggest that roughly half of American adults are overweight, a third are obese and women have grown particularly heavier in recent years. Across the world, the World Health Organisation estimates that 1.5 billion adults worldwide are overweight and 400 million are obese[11]. The highest rates of obesity are found in Mexico, Tunisia, the US, Saudi Arabia and Canada, and the lowest are found in China, Mali, Japan, Sweden and Brazil; the UK, Australia and New Zealand are all placed in the middle of the range. Across Europe, people in Northern and Western Europe are thinner than in Eastern and Southern Europe and women are more likely to be obese than men.

THE CONSEQUENCES OF BEING OVERWEIGHT

Obesity has several consequences and can cause both psychological and physical health problems.

Psychological problems

For children, the most immediate consequences of being overweight or obese are psychological, with many showing body dissatisfaction, low self esteem, anxiety, low mood and a general lack of confidence. Overweight children are also more likely to be bullied than thin children which can lead to under achievement or missing school. A similar pattern can also be seen with adults who also tend to show depression, anxiety, low self esteem and high levels of body dissatisfaction[11,12].

Physical problems

For children, the physical consequences of obesity mostly relate to being immobile and unfit and not being able to be as active as their peers. Some health problems do start early, however, and studies show a link between being obese as a child and having childhood asthma and Type 2 diabetes. For adults, obesity is clearly associated with a wide range of physical health problems including cardiovascular disease, heart attacks, diabetes, joint trauma, back pain, many types of cancer, hypertension and strokes, and the likelihood of these problems simply increases as a person's BMI gets greater than 25. The effects of obesity are also related to where the excess weight is carried, with weight stored around the middle of the body being more harmful than weight carried on the bottom or thighs. In the UK the prevalence of diabetes increased from 46% to 56% between 1996 and 2005, which can be largely explained by the rise in obesity. Obesity is also directly linked with mortality and decreased life expectancy[11,13].

THE CAUSES OF OVERWEIGHT

So what causes this problem? There are three key approaches to understanding the causes of weight gain: genetics, the environment and behaviour. Genetics and the environment will be considered in this chapter.

Genetics

Body size runs in families, and the probability that a child will be overweight is related to the parents' weight. For example, having one obese parent results in a 40% chance of a child being obese, and having two obese parents results in an 80% chance. In contrast, the probability that thin parents will produce overweight children is very small, about 7%. Parents and children, however, share both their environment and genetics, so this likeness could be due to either factor. To address this problem, research has examined twins and adoptees. The results show that the identical twins reared apart are more similar in weight than non-identical twins reared together, indicating a role for genetics. Studies also show that the weight of people who have been adopted is more similar to their biological parents than their adoptive family. In general, researchers believe that there is a role for genetics for both weight and where body fat is stored (upper versus lower body), that a mother's weight is a better predictor of her child's weight than that of the child's father and that the role of genetics gets less as a person's BMI gets larger[14].

But this cannot explain why there has been such a huge increase in the prevalence of obesity over the past 30 years, as our genes have not changed during this time. Nor can it explain the compelling evidence which comes from migration data which shows that as populations move from one country to the next, they quickly take on the body weight of their new environment[15]. For example, for Nigerians living in Nigeria, the prevalence of obesity is 5%, but for those Nigerians who move to the US, the rate is 39%. Similarly, for the Japanese living in Japan the rate of obesity is 4%, but for the Japanese living in Brazil the rate is also 39%. Finally, genetics cannot explain how obesity seems to be contagious within friendship groups. This has been studied using a social network approach which explores how BMI clusters within groups and shows that even though our body weight is similar to that of our parents, it is even more similar to that of our friends, and as our friends get fatter or thinner so do we[16].

Therefore, although it would seem that obesity runs in families and that some people might have a genetic predisposition to gain weight, genetics cannot be the main cause of this problem. Researchers have therefore turned to both the environment and individual behaviour as more useful explanations.

The obesogenic environment

To explain the increase in obesity, researchers have turned their attention to the role of the external world which has been labelled an 'obesogenic environment'[17]. For example, the food industry with its food advertising, cheap ready meals and takeaways discourages food shopping and cooking and encourages eating out and snacking. There has also been a reduction in manual labour and an increase in the use of cars, computers and TV which makes us more sedentary at both work and home. And even if we want to be active, lifts and escalators prevent stair use and towns are designed to make walking difficult due to the absence of street lights and pavements and large distances between homes and places of entertainment or shops. This obesogenic environment creates a world in which it is easy to gain weight and it requires effort to remain thin.

IN SUMMARY

The rates of obesity have increased worldwide since about the 1980s, and this has implications for physical and psychological health. Although there may be a role for genetics in the development of obesity, this cannot explain changes over time, the evidence from migration data or the impact of social networks and the weight of our friends. This points to the obesogenic environment, which makes it easy to gain weight and hard to remain thin. For me, however, this is not a sufficient explanation as not everyone living in an obesogenic environment becomes overweight. Therefore, there is also a clear role for two behaviours – eating and physical activity – which will be considered in the next two chapters.

3

WHY DO WE OVEREAT?

The energy in/energy out equation is a very fine balance, and even just eating one extra piece of toast per day that you don't need can result in a half stone increase in weight after a year. Imagine how quickly this could turn into becoming overweight or obese! It is clear, therefore, that people who are overweight have eaten more than they needed in the past. It is also clear that in order to maintain this level of weight, they must be eating exactly what they are using up in energy; otherwise their weight would go down. When asked why they eat, most people say, 'I'm hungry' or 'I like it', and they tend to see eating behaviour as a biological need driven by the need to survive. Eating behaviour however is much more complex than this as we eat for so many reasons other than hunger: 'I was bored', I was unhappy', 'It was there', 'I needed to clear my plate', 'Sunday lunch is a big family time', 'I was out with my friends'. At its simplest, eating can be seen as the result of what's in our heads and the triggers in our environment which in turn can lead to overeating.

WHAT'S IN OUR HEADS

From the moment we are born, we learn to like certain foods in the same way that we learn to speak, to like certain clothes or to enjoy certain hobbies. We learn through exposure and simply prefer the foods we are more familiar with. We learn by watching our parents, peers or the media and by seeing foods that others eat, particularly if those people are the ones we love or want to be like. And we learn through the simple process of reward and association. So if our parents said, 'Eat your vegetables and you can have pudding', 'You have been good, have a piece of cake', 'Have you had a difficult day? Have a biscuit' or 'Let's have a treat and go out for ice cream', we learn that sweet foods are treats and vegetables are boring and that treat foods make us feel special and are a great way to manage our emotions[18,19]. And this leaves us with a set of schema in our heads which we carry through into adulthood and use to determine what foods we like, when we eat and how much we eat. And these are the factors that cause overeating, which can be seen in terms of the following factors.

Emotional eating

When a child is upset, the easiest and quickest way to calm them down is to give them food. This acts as a distraction from the feelings they are having, gives them something to do with their hands and mouth and shifts their attention from whatever was upsetting them. If the food chosen is also seen as a treat such as sweets or a biscuit, then the child will feel 'treated' and happier. In the shorter term using food like this is effective. But in the longer term it can be harmful as we quickly learn that food is a good way to manage emotions. Then as we go through life, whenever we feel fed up, anxious or even just bored, we turn to food to make ourselves feel better. This is known as emotional eating, and studies indicate that emotional eating is linked with weight gain[20,21].

Social interaction

Food should be about hunger and fullness and seen as a simple fuel to keep the body going. Yet because of the way food is used in families and society in general, we develop a wide range of associations between food and other aspects of our lives. One of the key associations is between food and social interactions, and so for many people, food is not only about managing emotions but also about family time, birthdays, weddings, religious festivals, dating and the celebration of just about any occasion that involves being with other people. And for many this leads to overeating and subsequent weight gain.

Identity

Food also plays a central role in the way that we see ourselves and forms a core part of our identity. People therefore may see themselves as picky eaters, fussy or choosy about what they eat whilst others declare 'I eat anything'. Some become very health conscious and will only eat low fat, low sugar, low salt diets and turn to avoiding meat, additives and processed foods whilst others announce that nutritionists can't make their minds up about what we should eat and 'it's all nonsense' and therefore pride themselves in eating everything. And whilst some publicly proclaim 'I don't have much of an appetite these days', others proudly say 'I can eat like a horse'. These are all ways of using food as part of how we see ourselves and how we communicate who we are to the world around us. Food becomes a language to speak with and thus can result in eating more than we need and becoming overweight.

Guilt and denial

For some, food is a pleasure and a treat and part of the way in which they feel better about life. But for many, food is also linked with guilt and negativity. There is so much pressure to be thin with all its associations of attractiveness, control and emotional stability that people deny themselves food to lose weight. But then as this process of denial can only last so long, they end up eating and swing between eating, guilt about eating and subsequent overeating to manage the guilt. This in turn can lead to weight gain[22].

Food and reward

Food is linked with reward in many different ways. Eating food is rewarding as it tastes nice and makes us feel good. Food is also used as a reward for when we deserve a treat, take a break from work or have met one of our goals. And food can also be used a reward for eating or not eating food, as in 'I have finished my dinner so can have my pudding' or 'I have stuck to my diet and so deserve a piece of cake'. As a result unhealthy food often takes on the meaning of 'treat' whilst healthy food is seen as boring or just necessary. The problem for weight gain is that all of these rewards are in the here and now whereas the negative consequences of weight gain are always in the future. And people do 'future discounting' and so the benefits and rewards now always beat the costs in the future; cake now always beats a heart attack in 40 years, and so we overeat and our weight goes up[23,24].

A simple cost-benefit analysis

At its simplest, eating behaviour is really a cost-benefit analysis with people weighing up the benefits (managing emotions, being sociable, making a statement about identity, pleasure and reward) against the costs (guilt, risk, obesity, diabetes, heart disease). Unfortunately, when it comes to food, most of the benefits are in the here and now and most of the costs are in the future, which means that the benefits mostly win and people ending eating more than they should.

Eating is therefore a response to how we think about food. Eating is also a response to triggers in our environment.

TRIGGERS IN OUR ENVIRONMENT

The obesogenic environment makes it very easy to eat and offers a wide range of triggers which cause mindless eating and change what, when, where, how and why we eat.

Mindless eating

Bags of crisps used to be 30 g and we would eat these and stop. Many bags are now 'grab bags' and are 60 g. Very few people eat the original 30 g and then stop; they eat the lot – twice the amount they used to eat. We now live in a world where portion sizes are bigger, cakes are offered around at work, we have snacks in our cupboards and 'drive in' fast food restaurants where we can buy thousands of calories' worth of food without even having to stop driving to eat it. And we eat it not because we are hungrier than we used to be but because it's there. And when we are eating it, we do so without realising that we are eating, and as a result it doesn't make us full. This is known as mindless eating[25]. Recently we did a study looking at how much people ate in four different situations: in the car, watching TV, chatting to someone or on their own. We found two results[26]. First, people ate more whilst watching TV than in any of the other situations, which also has been found in many other studies[27]. Second, the amount they ate whilst driving was unrelated to changes in their hunger. This indicates that we eat more when we are distracted, particularly when watching TV. It also indicates that if we are distracted, as when we are driving, we don't register the food we have eaten and it doesn't make us full. In turn, this has also been shown to lead to even more eating later on[28]. Such mindless eating makes people overeat in an environment where food is easily available, and over time this causes weight gain.

What we eat

With the decrease in cooking from scratch and the increase in fast food outlets, takeaways and ready meals, the obesogenic environment has changed what we eat. This causes weight gain as fast foods, takeaways and ready meals are often very high in fat, and one theory of obesity is that it is linked to a diet relatively high in fat compared to carbohydrates. To support this theory, a study of 11,500 people in Scotland showed that those men and women who ate the lowest proportion of carbohydrate in their diets were up to four times more likely to be obese than those eating the highest proportion of carbohydrate[29]. A similar study in Leeds also provided support for the fat proportion theory of obesity[30]. This study reported that high fat eaters who derived more than 45% of their energy from fat were 19 times more likely to be obese than those who derived less than 35% of their energy from fat. A diet relatively high in fat may cause weight gain and obesity as it takes more energy to burn carbohydrates than fat. Carbohydrates are burned and fat is stored; carbohydrates make you feel full faster and fat does not switch off the desire to eat, making it easier to eat more and more fat without feeling full.

When we eat

The obesogenic environment also means that we are far more likely to eat snacks than meals and unfortunately, snacks are often higher in fat and calories and more likely to be forgotten or discounted. So if you ask someone what they ate yesterday, they will tell you their breakfast, lunch and dinner but not the snacks (or drinks) in between. This means that snacking makes people eat more in the longer term as they have not registered that they have eaten and therefore don't feel as full. There is also some evidence that those who are overweight may be more likely to skip meals, particularly breakfast, which may make them more likely to snack throughout the rest of the day[31].

Where we eat

There have also been changes to where people eat, and not only do people eat more snacks but they also eat these snacks on the go, either in the car, at their desks or in the street. We recently did a study of the impact of 'eating on the go' and found that those who ate a cereal bar whilst walking around the corridors of the university consumed more later on than those who ate the cereal bar sitting down at a table. Eating on the go seemed to make people feel less full afterwards, meaning that they carried on eating when food was made available again[32]. And then, when people do sit down to eat, they often eat in front of the TV, which can also increase food intake[27]. This is because they are distracted from eating and so don't notice how much they have consumed.

How we eat

There is also some evidence that weight gain may be related to how we eat with obese people tending to show a faster initial rate of eating and to take larger spoonfuls of food[33]. This may be because they are eating food as snacks, eating on the go rather than as a meal or due to higher levels of emotional eating which makes them anxious around food.

Why we eat

Ideally we would eat when we are hungry and stop when we are full. But as described above, we eat for many other reasons as food is used a way to manage our emotions, for social interaction, to make statements of our identity – all the factors that are in our heads. The environment around us not only changes when, where, what and how we eat; it also changes why we eat, and it also acts as a trigger for these different reasons. So if food is there we eat mindlessly, rather than when we are hungry. But if the environment triggers our emotions, we eat for emotional regulation; if we are in a café, we eat for social interaction; if we are with certain people in our lives, we eat to make a statement about how we want these people to see us.

IN SUMMARY

At its simplest, weight gain is a result of us eating more than we need. This chapter has explored the reasons why people overeat with a focus on what's in our heads and the triggers in our environment. It has also shown that at times, these triggers in our environment then change which part of what's in our heads is most important. And this can all lead to weight gain.

4

WHY ARE WE NOT ACTIVE ENOUGH?

The energy in/energy out equation highlights an equal role for activity. In fact, one study explored the relationship between body weight and floor of residence in nearly 3,000 normal weight adults across eight European cities[34]. The results showed that for men, living on a higher floor was associated with lower BMI. The authors concluded that daily stair climbing may reduce weight and therefore should be encouraged. The Department of Health recommends that adults do at least 30 minutes of exercise on five or more days a week, yet many people live very sedentary lifestyles and do not manage this. Why people do or do not do exercise can also be understood in terms of what is in our heads and the triggers in the environment.

WHAT'S IN OUR HEADS

Exercise and being physically active in daily life has many consequences. For example, it is clear that being more active is linked with feeling more energetic; a reduction in the risk for diseases such as cancer, diabetes, obesity, heart attacks and strokes; and an increase in life expectancy. Further, it also has an impact on numerous psychological factors with exercise resulting in improved mood, confidence and self esteem and a reduction in depression and anxiety. But knowing these outcomes does not always make people be more active as deciding to do exercise and then actually doing it is related to the way in which we think, as follows.

Social contact

It has long been recognised that one of the main reasons why people do exercise is that it provides social contact[35]. This is why group sports such as football, basketball and netball are popular with children. It is also why adults join gyms: to attend dance, aerobic or spinning classes so that they can exercise whilst being with other people. Exercise is more likely to happen if it is a social activity which brings with it social benefits. Not recognising or valuing the social benefits of exercise may lead to people becoming inactive, which in turn can prompt weight gain.

Social norms

Exercise also reflects whether being active is the norm in someone's family or social group. Research shows that body weight is 'contagious' and that friends tend to have a similar body weight to each other. This suggests that a norm of body weight has been established within these friendship groups, and over time people within the group change their weight to be more similar to that norm. In a similar vein, being active also runs in families and between friends. So if you change jobs and make new friends who are all quite active, chances are that you will become more active as well. Similarly, if you meet a group of people who enjoy sitting around eating cake and drinking tea, then you may well start to gain weight. Such social norms therefore influence how active people become.

Exercise is fun

Most exercise campaigns emphasise health benefits and tell people that keeping active is good for your heart, helps you live longer and helps you to maintain a healthy weight. But most of this means very little to most people who live in the present and find it hard to worry about having a heart attack when they are 65. We are very bad at 'future thinking' and only really concerned with the here and now. Therefore, the next main reason why people exercise is having fun. If exercise is fun, the benefits of doing it now easily outweigh the costs, and it works by making the here and now more enjoyable. And believing it is fun can make people start to be more active.

The impact of exercise on mood

There is strong evidence that exercise is good for our mood[36]. This may take the form of a 'runners high' for those who are very fit but for most people it's just a sense of happiness, being alive and a release of stress when we are outdoors, in the fresh air and being active. Once people have felt the psychological benefits of exercise, they will start to believe that being active benefits them and therefore will do more of it.

Confidence

Feeling confident is also key to being active. This can involve being confident at sports such as swimming, basketball, football or tennis. It can also mean feeling confident that you know where the changing rooms are at the local leisure centre, knowing how to pay to get in, knowing where to get the bus from or knowing the route to walk to school. The best way to build confidence is simply to do something a few times, congratulate yourself on having done it and then do it more.

Embarrassment

Being active can involve getting sweaty, breathless and red in the face, wearing close-fitting fabrics, having your body wobble in public and getting undressed in a changing room. All of these factors, and even the anticipation of these, can make people feel embarrassed and therefore remain at home and inactive.

The perceived costs of exercise

Given that we live very much in the moment, at the time of choosing to be active, the benefits at that time need to outweigh the costs. There are, however, many costs that get in the way, and people may say, 'It's time consuming', 'It's boring', 'I'm busy', 'I don't like getting sweaty', 'I don't like having to change clothes', 'It's embarrassing as I'm not very fit' and 'It costs too much to join a gym'. Exercise will be more likely to happen if it is done in a way that avoids all these costs.

Habit

The best predictor of how we will behave in the future is how we have behaved in the past. All the beliefs described above will increase the likelihood that someone will be more active. Then, once they have started to be more active, a habit will be established which becomes increasingly difficult to break.

Valuing health

For most people, being healthy is not a powerful motivator as it is too far in the future, and the immediate benefits of being unhealthy (eating cake now, watching TV now) will always win over something in 5 or even 10 years' time. But some degree of valuing health is bound to influence how we behave. For many, their health becomes more of a motivator once they develop symptoms such as breathlessness, aches and pains, a lack of energy or just a feeling of getting older. This can then prompt a determination to become more active.

All of these factors are 'in our heads' and reflect the schemas we have developed over the course of our lives. These in turn influence how active we are, which in turn will change our body weight.

TRIGGERS IN THE ENVIRONMENT

Being active and exercising is also a response to triggers in the environment, and in the same way an obesogenic environment makes it easy to overeat, it also encourages us to do less. These triggers can change our level of activity in the following ways.

Accessibility

Being active requires green spaces, pavements, cycle paths, stairs, gyms, sports facilities and playgrounds. Simply having access to these facilities makes it much more likely that someone will be active.

Cost and time

Any barriers to exercise will deter people from being more active, and these can include the financial cost of gym membership and the time needed to travel to a place of exercise and get changed and showered. Therefore high prices, facilities that are difficult to reach and busy lives can provide a barrier to becoming more active.

Part of daily life

The main reason for being active is that it is 'just part of my life'. Therefore, if children walk to school, play in the garden, climb trees, cycle to their friend's house or play active games at home (rather than sitting in front of the TV or computer), they will be exercising without knowing it and staying healthy with the minimum amount of effort. Similarly, if adults walk to work or at least use public transport, use stairs rather than lifts, walk up escalators, walk to the shops or out for the evening and minimize the amount of time spent sitting at home or work, they too will be doing exercise without having to think about it. Accordingly, an environment that makes it easier to incorporate activity into everyone's daily life will be more likely to trigger more active lifestyles.

Low effort

At its simplest, exercise is the response to a cost-benefit analysis of the pros and cons of being active. Often what makes people carry out any activity is that it is low effort in terms of time, money, emotion and thinking. The environment can contribute to this by making exercise either higher or lower effort depending upon what is offered to each individual.

IN SUMMARY

This chapter has outlined the causes of physical activity, and like eating behaviour, this is also linked to what's in our heads and the triggers in our environment. Any attempt at weight loss has to address these factors.

5

DIETING AND ITS CONSEQUENCES

Dieting comes in many forms and has positive and negative consequences for the dieter. This chapter will describe what dieting is and when people diet. It will then explore the impact of dieting on physical factors such as weight, health status and mortality and psychological factors such as mood, eating behaviour and identity. It also covers the ways in which dieting remains central to the medical and surgical management of obesity.

WHAT IS DIETING?

Since about the 1960s there has been an endless stream of new diets on the market, including those recommending eating only fruit, only meat or only meal substitute drinks; those excluding whole food groups such as carbohydrates, fats, protein or sugars; and those recommending missing meals, calorie counting, a points system, having days on and days off or following a healthy eating meal plan. A recent international study explored the many different ways that people use to try to lose weight and maintain this weight loss and identified a wide range of strategies[37]. This large-scale study identified 37 weight loss strategies, the most common being eating more fruit and vegetables, selecting food more consciously, eating soup and self weighing.

Further, the researchers also identified 12 motivations, of which the most common were to improve well-being, to improve health and prevent disease and to improve fitness and appearance. But whatever the method, at its essence a diet is anything that suggests that you eat less than you usually would and impose some level of control over your eating in order to lose weight. Studies have also explored the prevalence of dieting and indicate that about 42% of the general population report trying to lose weight in the past year, about 23% report trying to maintain weight loss in the past year and about 70% report having ever dieted to lose weight[37]. There are several reasons why people diet, which will now be addressed.

WHY DO PEOPLE DIET?

The three key reasons why people diet are to lose weight when they are overweight, as a response to body dissatisfaction and as part of a need to regain control as shown by those with eating disorders.

When overweight people want to lose weight

Those who are overweight or obese diet as a means to lose weight. For some, this involves joining a formal weight management group either via a referral from their doctor or simply by attending on their own. For many, however, it involves self imposed limits which may be guided through diet books, the internet, apps or self help groups. Dieting is also an intrinsic part of the medical and surgical management of overweight.

When dieting alone has failed, overweight or obese people can turn to medication and as Hirsch said in 1998, 'Who would not rejoice to find a magic bullet that we could fire into obese people to make them permanently slim and healthy?'[38]. Doctors have been offering weight loss drugs for many years and often used to prescribe amphetamines, which was stopped due to the drug's addictive qualities. Nowadays, drug therapy is only legally available to patients in the UK with a BMI of 30 or more, and government bodies have become increasingly restrictive on the use of anti-obesity drugs.

There are currently two groups of anti-obesity drugs offered in conjunction with dietary and exercise programmes. Those in the first group suppress appetite. Although there is some evidence for the effectiveness of these drugs, they can also be accompanied by side effects such as nausea, dry mouth and constipation. Recently all of these drugs have been removed from the market due to the risk of heart attacks and lowered mood. The second group of drugs reduce fat absorption. Orlistat is one of these and can cause weight loss in obese subjects. It is, however, accompanied by a range of unpleasant side effects, including liquid stools, an urgent need to go to the toilet and anal leakage, which are particularly apparent following a high fat meal as the fat is blocked from entering the blood stream. At present there is an over-the-counter version of Orlistat which is a lower dose than that prescribed by the doctor but has a similar effect. We have carried out research into the impact of Orlistat which indicates that when it works, it does so by making obese people realise that their weight is caused by what they eat rather than their biological makeup, as simply seeing the fat in their diet come out in such an unpleasant way helps them make the link between fat eaten and fat stored in the body. They then change their diet[39,40]. This medical approach to weight can therefore only work if people also diet at the same time. Unfortunately, people sometimes eat a high fat diet, see the unpleasant consequences and just stop taking the drugs rather than changing their diet.

Many people are also turning to obesity surgery. In the UK, the US and most European countries, surgery is available for those with a BMI greater than 40, or greater than 35 if they have other health problems such as diabetes or hypertension. Although there are 21 different surgical procedures for obesity, the two most popular are the Roux en Y gastric bypass and gastric banding. Research indicates that weight loss surgery is effective for both weight loss and weight loss maintenance and can reduce the risk of heart disease and switch off diabetes[41,42]. It is not all good news, however, as some individuals who have surgery do not lose as much weight as expected or show weight regain[43]. They may also lose weight too quickly and become malnourished. In addition, some are left with large amounts of excess skin which is difficult to manage and requires further plastic surgery. My research on the psychological effects of obesity surgery indicate that not only does weight loss cause improved self esteem and confidence, which you would expect from any effective weight loss method, but people also felt less hungry, less preoccupied with food and more in control of their eating behaviour. I have called this 'the paradox of control' as by taking away control from the individual, they paradoxically feel more in control[44]. Surgery, however, still requires some level of dieting and it is becoming clear that longer term weight loss maintenance after surgery requires people to control their own food intake instead of relying upon the limits imposed by the surgery itself.

Dieting as a response to body disatisfaction

Although many people diet as a means to improve their health, the more immediate goal is often to improve their body satisfaction. And whilst some with body disatisfaction may be overweight, many are not but are critical of the way they look. Body disatisfaction can also be a key driver of dieting behaviour but is not always a healthy one.

What is body disatisfaction?

Body dissatisfaction can be conceptualised in three different ways. First it can be seen as a discrepancy between individuals' perception of their body size and their real body size, which can be detected using distorting mirrors or a system of lights to assess how large someone's body really is compared to how large they think it is. Second it is sometimes measured as the discrepancy between how someone perceives their body size compared to their ideal body size. Third it may simply be feelings of discontent with the body's size and shape and a sense that one's thighs are too wobbly or one's breasts are too small[45]. So who shows body dissatisfaction?

The prevalence of body dissatisfaction

In general women are more dissatisfied with their bodies than men and would prefer their chests to be larger and their legs, stomachs, hips, thighs, bottoms and overall body shape to be smaller. But men also show body dissatisfaction. Research indicates that men are primarily worried about their penis size, body weight and height, and that their overall appearance self esteem was related to their satisfaction with their weight, muscularity, height and penis size. Further, studies suggest that in general men would prefer their arms, chests and shoulders to be larger and their stomachs and overall body to be smaller. Although those with an eating disorder or weight problem show body dissatisfaction, it has become increasingly clear that body dissatisfaction is common amongst people of all shapes and sizes[45.]

Causes of body dissatisfaction

There are many possible causes of body dissatisfaction, but the most likely culprits are the media and the home environment.

The most commonly held belief in both the lay and academic communities is that body dissatisfaction is a response to representations of 'ideal bodies' in the media. Magazines, newspapers, television, films and even novels predominantly use images of thin women to sell to women and images of muscular men to sell to men. At times these models may be advertising body size–related items such as food and clothes, but often they promote neutral items such as vacuum cleaners and wallpaper. Research indicates that through the processes of social comparison and internalisation, normal people accept these ideal images and become critical of the way they look. In fact, research shows that even after a brief exposure to such images in an experiment, women, in particular, end up feeling worse about their appearance[46,47].

Research has also explored the impact of the home environment on body dissatisfaction and indicates a key role for the mother's own body dissatisfaction on that of her daughter as well as the mother-daughter relationship. In particular, studies indicate that mothers who are dissatisfied with their own bodies communicate this to their daughters, which results in the daughters' own body dissatisfaction[48]. Furthermore, mother-daughter relationships which are overly enmeshed or which limit the daughter's own autonomy may also promote body dissatisfaction in the daughter together with a mother who is critical of the way her daughter looks. There is less research on the communication of body dissatisfaction for men, but it is likely that a similar pattern exists with a father who is critical of either his own body or that of his son, being more likely to create a son who is also dissatisfied with how he looks.

Dieting as a part of an eating disorder

Dieting is also core to eating disorders and can be very problematic. There are many different eating disorders (EDs), including anorexia nervosa (AN; excessive weight loss), bulimia nervosa (BN; bingeing and purging), binge eating disorder (BED; binge eating but without purging), orthorexia (excessive concern about healthy eating) and eating disorder not otherwise specified (EDNOS), a general term for other forms of EDs which don't quite fulfill the criteria for other problems[49]. This section will focus on AN and BN as they tend to be the most well-known disorders and often generate the most concern. Many of their characteristics, however, are also relevant to other forms of EDs. Research has addressed what EDs are and the role of a number of factors in their development.

What are EDs?

AN affects about 1% of girls and women in the Western world, and although the prevalence of AN increased dramatically between the 1960s and 1990s, it appears to have become more stable over recent years. There are generally two types of AN: restricting anorexia, which involves food restriction and no episodes of bingeing or purging, and binge eating anorexia, which involves both food restriction and episodes of bingeing or purging through self induced vomiting or the misuse of laxatives, diuretics or enemas. BN affects about twice as many people as AN, although many people with BN do not come into contact with health professionals as it is a much more private disorder with sufferers often managing to carry on an apparently normal life. Those with BN are usually within the normal weight range and maintain this weight through the processes of bingeing and purging. EDs have serious health implications and whilst AN has a high mortality rate due to malnutrition (higher than any other psychiatric problem) and is associated with problems with the cardiovascular and nervous system, depression and anxiety, BN is linked with suicide, addictions and digestive problems. All people with EDs, including AN and BN, restrict their food intake as a means to control their weight and therefore dieting is a key part of their behaviour.

The causes of EDs

Some research has highlighted a role for genetics, although the impact of genetics is by no means clear cut and many people with an ED have no family history whatsoever. Other research has highlighted a role for family dynamics emphasising enmeshed relationships, poor boundaries and the key role of mothers. Further, some theories emphasise the symptoms of EDs as a form of communication in which those with EDs use their weight loss, starvation and extreme food avoidance as a means to communicate that something is wrong. Another theory highlights the role of faulty thinking and issues of control and perfectionism with people showing black and white thinking and a belief that unless they can control their weight, they will have no control at all.

The most commonly held lay theory about EDs, however, is that they are a product of body dissatisfaction, probably caused by the media which triggers dieting behaviour. In line with this it is argued that the weight loss caused by dieting is then reinforced either by others ('You have lost weight') or a feeling of power and control ('I have achieved something'), which means that the person finds it difficult to stop[50]. The evidence does indicate that most people who develop an ED do show body dissatisfaction and have dieted in the past, so there clearly is a link. Evidence also shows, however, that the vast majority of those who experience body dissatisfaction and then diet do not go on to develop an ED. Eating disorders are therefore clearly linked with dieting as restricting food intake plays a key role in these problems and can sometimes contribute to the onset of an ED. There are also a multitude of other factors that also contribute to an ED with dieting only being one of many.

People therefore diet for many reasons. All of these approaches to dieting have implications for physical and psychological health and well-being.

PHYSICAL HEALTH CONSEQUENCES

Dieting changes our physical health in a number of ways.

Weight loss

If effective, dieting can lead to weight loss, and evidence indicates that about 60% of people who diet lose weight in the first six months. This is increased to about 70% with some form of sustained follow-up from a health professional. A recent review of the evidence by NICE, however, indicated that by one year, those who had received best case behavioural management from either public sector or private sector weight management behaviour change services such as the NHS, Weight Watchers or Slimming World showed an average weight loss of 2.22 kg[51]. Similarly, a review of those interventions focusing on food intake and physical activity showed an average of 1.56 kg less weight regain by one year compared to controls[52]. Further, a trial of those referred to a commercial weight loss company through the NHS indicated that whilst two thirds lost less than 5% of their body weight, one third lost more than 5% after at least starting a 12-week course[53]. There is always variation around these figures, however, with some people losing more weight and some losing less. In terms of surgery, research uses percentage of excess weight loss or change in BMI as the main outcome measure and indicates that by one year, the mean percentage of excess weight loss is about 40% for a gastric band and 60% for Roux en Y gastric bypass. By 10 years, this has reduced to about 50% excess weight loss with about 10–20% of patients showing significant weight regain[41,54]. For medication combined with behavioural modification, by one year follow-up, the average weight loss is 1.8 kg greater than a placebo control group[52].

Health status

Although weight losses can seem small following dieting attempts, evidence indicates that when people are overweight, even 10% weight loss causes a dramatic reduction in the risk of heart disease and stroke, a reversal of Type 2 diabetes so that a person can start to regulate their own blood sugars again and a reduction in the risk of weight-related cancers such as breast cancer and endometrial cancer in women[55,56].

Mortality

Being overweight is strongly linked to shorter life expectancy. Losing weight can improve life expectancy as long as this weight loss is sustained.

Symptoms

Regardless of mortality and more serious health conditions, weight loss can also improve a person's daily physical health through the reduction of symptoms such as breathlessness, back and knee pain and the susceptibility to minor infections.

Yo-yo dieting and weight regain

Unfortunately, although the majority of people who diet manage to lose weight initially, many show weight regain by a five-year follow-up. Some research suggests that having some periods of time in your life when you weigh less, even if this weight is regained, may be healthier in the same way that stopping smoking for the odd month or even year gives the lungs time to recover[56]. Other research indicates, however, that yo-yo dieting (i.e. showing large fluctuations in weight) may be harmful – even more harmful than remaining at a more stable higher weight[57]. This is because when a person loses weight, they often lose muscle and fat, but when they put it back on, they regain proportionally more fat, making them not only heavier but fatter over time. In turn this has a negative impact on their cardiovascular health, can add to fatty liver disease and exacerbates their risk of diabetes. It would be a shame if this deterred people from trying to lose weight, but it does indicate the negative side of failed dieting.

PSYCHOLOGICAL HEALTH CONSEQUENCES

Dieting also has many psychological consequences, and again, this often depends on whether dieting leads to weight loss and whether this weight loss is sustained.

Mood, confidence and body image

Weight loss can lead to improved mood and a reduction in anxiety and depression. Those who lose weight also report increases in self confidence and body image, although this can sometimes take time as people need to internalise their new body size and sometimes report buying clothes that are too large whilst they learn to come to terms with their body shape. When weight is regained, however, these improvements are seldom sustained with people sometimes reporting feeling worse than before as they see themselves as having failed and let themselves down.

Identity

When dieting is successful, many people describe a sense of being 'reborn', of having 'a second chance', or being a 'new person' and feeling 'liberated'. This shift in identity can result in a change of job, a new relationship or a determination to live life to the fullest. It sometimes also leads to people becoming a spokesperson for weight loss, to setting up their own dieting company or to becoming very passionate about exercise and healthy eating. Interestingly, those who show such a shift in their identity also seem more likely to keep their weight off in the longer term as they have more invested in success.

Preoccupation with food

At its heart, dieting involves not eating food that people want to eat, and whether this involves avoiding whole food groups, eating fewer calories or just eating less, it always involves some level of denial. As a result, many dieters develop a preoccupation with the very thing they are trying not to have: food. This is parallel to 'the theory of ironic processes of mental control' described by Wegner. For his initial study, he asked groups of people to either think about a white bear or *not* to think about a white bear and then to ring a bell if they had that thought. Predictably, those who were told not to think about the white bear rang their bell more[58]. This has been called a paradoxical effect as trying not to think about something makes people think about it more and is exactly what happens to a lot of people when they diet. For the majority, the preoccupation with food takes the form of thinking about food for a disproportionate amount of time. For others this can become more pathological, leading to EDs such as AN or BN.

Overeating

At times dieting can result in people eating less and losing weight. But for many, trying to eat less often results in people eating more. This may be in the form of compensatory overeating when people simply eat the amount or types of foods they have been avoiding. At times, however, this can also result in binge eating. This has been called the 'what the hell' effect and occurs when people feel that they have broken their diet through eating a food that was not allowed, when they have low mood and overeat to cheer themselves up, or after drinking alcohol when their resistance is lowered[59]. Such overeating can then make people feel worse about themselves, which in turn can lower self esteem and trigger guilt, which may lead to further overeating as people use food to manage their emotions.

IN SUMMARY

Dieting involves trying to eat less as a means to lose weight and can be a response to being overweight or obese, body dissatisfaction or even an ED. Dieting has implications for both physical and psychological health, and when it is effective, people show improvements in their risks for diseases such as heart disease and diabetes and a reduction in symptoms such as breathlessness and joint pain. They can also experience improved mood and body satisfaction. At times, dieting can lead to weight loss followed by weight regain, which may be worse for health than just remaining overweight. It can also trigger a preoccupation with food and overeating. This raises the questions 'Why do diets fail?' and 'When do diets succeed?' These questions will be addressed in the next two chapters.

6

WHY DO DIETS FAIL?

Changing eating behaviour involves changing what's in our heads and managing our environment to promote eating less and doing more. But many diets fail because eating is a habit and habits are hard to change. This chapter will explore how habits are formed, why eating habits are so hard to change and the reasons for failed dieting, both in terms emotional triggers, of what's in our heads and factors in the environment such as physical triggers and social pressure.

HOW ARE EATING HABITS FORMED?

Habits are formed through four very simple processes: modelling, repetition, reinforcement and association. We often carry out a behaviour because we see other people doing it. When we repeat a behaviour several times, it becomes a pattern. It then becomes a habit if it is reinforced by something positive such as the fact that we like it, that someone else likes us doing it and that it makes us feel good. This is even true for 'bad habits' as these also make us feel good at some level. A habit becomes a strong habit if it is associated with something in our environment or our mood[60,61]. For example, take breakfast. Lots of people don't like breakfast as they are 'too tired', or they say, 'It makes me feel sick' or 'I just can't eat in the morning'. This is because their normal behaviour is not to eat and eating first thing in the morning feels strange. But then if someone eats breakfast in front of them and if some factor can get them to eat breakfast every morning for a couple of weeks, a new pattern will soon be set (repetition). They will start to like the feeling of being more alert and will spend a few minutes each morning sitting quietly eating breakfast (reinforcement), and this new behaviour will be triggered by seeing the fridge, smelling someone else's toast or simply getting out of bed (association). Not eating breakfast will then start to feel strange as their new normal behaviour has been established.

These habits are all established from a very early age and become so entrenched in our daily lives and the things we say about ourselves that they require very little thought or effort to do but a lot of effort to change.

WHY ARE HABITS DIFFICULT TO CHANGE?

Habits are difficult to change as ultimately, at the moment of doing any behaviour, its benefits outweigh the costs. So, although eating cake may add to your weight problem, at the time of eating cake, the pleasure of its taste and texture cancel out the fear of having a heart attack when you are 60. Habits are therefore the result of a simple cost-benefit analysis, and mostly, we are hopeless at thinking about the future, so the immediate benefits pretty much always outweigh the future costs. This process is facilitated by a number of different factors, as follows, which are either in our heads or in the environment.

What's in our heads

There are many factors inside our heads that make eating habits hard to change.

Emotional triggers: Because habits have been created by associating the behaviour with a number of triggers, they are difficult to break as every time we come across this trigger we are prompted to behave in a particular way. Some of these triggers are in our heads such as our mood (e.g. feeling fed up) and are therefore very difficult to avoid as they follow us everywhere and are hard to ignore. And because habits require so little thought, much of the time we aren't even aware of what we are doing or how our emotions are determining what foods we eat.

Withdrawal and feelings of worry and stress: Habits are part of our everyday lives and therefore, when we don't clean our teeth, eat breakfast, have our morning coffee or have biscuits in the afternoon, we feel unsettled and a little bit stressed. This feeling is unpleasant and we quickly learn that it can be avoided by carrying on with our habit. Therefore, not eating biscuits feels unusual, but this can all be made OK with a few biscuits. And the habit carries on as it becomes the solution to the problem created when trying to change it. It's a vicious circle. But it's the change in the habit which makes us feel stressed, not the absence of the actual behaviour. And if we start to realise that the feeling of stress or worry is just 'withdrawal' and will only be made worse in the longer term if we give in and use the habit to get rid of it, then we can start to break the habit itself.

Scripts in our heads: From an early age we develop scripts in our heads of what we like and don't like, who we are and what we do. These scripts come from the people around us, particularly our parents, and tell us whether we are a good or bad person. For example, some people have negative scripts in their heads which say, 'I am always late', 'I'm a problem', 'I'm selfish', 'I never try my best' or 'I'm stupid'. Other people may have more positive scripts which tell them 'I am kind', 'I am thoughtful', 'I work hard', 'I always stick at things' and 'I'm clever'. In terms of eating habits, these scripts can make it very difficult to change if we tell ourselves, 'I have a problem with food', 'Eating is my only crutch in life' or 'I have an addictive personality'. Although some of these scripts may feel 'true' and reflect how people actually behave, they make it more difficult to change as breaking a long-standing habit not only means changing the behaviour but also changing the very way in which a person sees themselves. And this is hard.

Denial and rebound effects: When people try to change their habits, they are mostly attempting to stop doing something they still want to do. So people on a diet like chips but try not to eat them, and those trying to be active would rather be on the sofa but try to drag themselves off to an exercise class. This makes changing behaviour difficult because it always introduces an element of denial and human beings are hopeless at denying themselves something if they want it and it is available. Furthermore, the process of denial makes the behaviour we are trying to deny ourselves even more attractive and desirable than it was before, which can create rebound effects. So if we say to ourselves, 'Today I will not eat cake', automatically we think about cake more, not less. Then, because we are thinking about cake more but can't have it, we want it more as the day progresses. Eventually when we give in and have cake, not only do we now want it more than we did in the morning, we end up eating more cake because we have been denying ourselves all day. This is a very powerful effect which means that by making food forbidden and putting ourselves into denial, we paradoxically become more preoccupied, and when we do give in (which most people do), we paradoxically eat more than if we hadn't denied ourselves in the first place. This is called the 'what the hell' effect[59].

A challenged identity: Although people who are overweight may not like being overweight and want to be thinner, their identity can often be tied up with their body size. When they first start to lose weight, this can be rewarding as they may feel healthier and can see their body shape changing. But with this comes a challenge to their identity as they will feel pressure from themselves and others to be someone different. At this point some people 'sabotage' their diets as the new thinner version of themselves can be perceived as a threat. This can lead to overeating and weight regain.

Beliefs about food preferences: Food preferences are learned from the moment we are born through exposure to different foods, learning by modelling and watching others and the association between different foods and certain places and feelings. Our food preferences are therefore embedded and feel as if they are fixed in a pattern on our tongues. Dieting can involve eating less of the foods we usually eat. But sometimes it may involve trying new foods, which can be a challenge to our beliefs about the food we like or dislike. So if we snack on chocolate or cake in the afternoon, dieting may just involve cutting this out. And if we eat large portions of spaghetti bolognaise for our dinner, then a diet would involve a smaller portion. But a diet may also involve finding a substitute for the chocolate or cake, such as fruit, and if we eat lots of chips, then a diet might involve eating rice or boiled potatoes instead. Yet if we believe that we don't like these foods, then the diet will be hard to follow. And the new healthier habits will be harder to set up.

Cross addiction: Many people use food to regulate their emotions, and when they are dieting, they need to find an alternative source of support. Ideally this would be through exercise, talking to friends, going to the cinema or reading a book. But some need to have a more substantial substitute and this can lead to cross addiction. Research on the impact of obesity surgery indicates that patients can develop a range of addictions after surgery, including smoking, alcoholism, shopping or sex addiction. In terms of weight loss, some of these are probably quite useful but alcohol contains large amounts of hidden calories and can undermine dieting attempts, causing weight regain. It may also lead to the 'what the hell' effect if people become disinhibited and therefore overeat.

Eating habits are therefore hard to change due to a number of factors inside our heads. Such change is also hindered by triggers in the environment.

Triggers in the environment

Eating becomes associated with many different aspects of our environment which can prompt eating even we are trying to eat less.

Physical triggers

Some environmental triggers are physical, such as the biscuit tin, the fridge, carefully placed snack foods in supermarkets or the cake trolley at work, which cause mindless shopping and mindless eating. Yet as with emotional triggers, much of this habitual behaviour is done without thinking; those who overeat and eat biscuits with their afternoon cup of tea do so as this feels normal and not doing so doesn't feel quite right. Such physical triggers, however, unlike emotional triggers can be avoided if we make small changes to our daily routines or change our environment.

Social pressure

Our behaviours are intricately linked with other people and are often central to how we build up our relationships. So we may have a friend at work with whom we have cake in the afternoon, a husband who likes to buy us chocolates as a treat or children who we enjoy taking out for ice cream. If we then try to change our behaviour, these other people in our lives may object and the pressure is on to behave the way we always have done. Husbands will feel rejected if we don't eat the chocolates, our friend will feel lonely eating cake on their own and we will miss out on the gossip and ice cream will seem less of a treat. People like us to carry on the way we always have done as it makes them feel safe. If we change, then they feel that they have to change, and that is unsettling. So the social pressure always increases to maintain the status quo whenever anyone tries to break a habit. I remember a woman once who was part of my research and trying to lose weight. Her rather unpleasant husband wanted her to lose weight and used to say 'Here comes the elephant' when she got ready for bed. She went on a diet and was doing really well. He started to buy her chocolates. I think she left him.

IN SUMMARY

Habits are a product of modelling, repetition, reinforcement and association and are difficult to change because they have often been entrenched for a very long time. They illustrate a simple cost-benefit analysis and at the time of carrying out the behaviour, the immediate benefits will always outweigh the longer term costs. This means that diets often fail as people are unable to change these habits. In addition, changing eating habits is made even more difficult due to factors such as emotional triggers, denial and withdrawal and environmental triggers which prompt mindless eating or social pressure from others who want us to carry on as usual. But sometimes diets work! This is addressed in the next chapter.

7

SUCCESSFUL DIETING

Although dieting is hard, some people do succeed. Research has taken three different approaches to explore why some people manage to lose weight and keep it off. First, some studies have identified success stories and used qualitative methods to explore how these people have managed to show weight loss maintenance. Second, other studies have used quantitative methods to compare those who have been successful to those who have been less successful. Finally, some studies have taken the data from large-scale interventions to explore what factors predict weight loss maintenance in the longer term. This chapter will describe the results from these three different approaches and then pull them together to find common themes that form the basis of successful dieting.

APPROACH 1: SUCCESS STORIES

Over the past few years researchers have conducted a series of qualitative studies with in-depth interviews to explore the accounts of those who have lost weight and kept it off. These stories indicate the kinds of factors associated with success[39,62–66].

Life events

Successful weight loss and weight loss maintenance often seem to happen after people have had a life event of some sort. People have called these events many things, such as 'seeing the light', 'an epiphany', 'reaching rock bottom', 'a tipping point' or just a time when the normal pattern of life is shaken up and habits can be broken more easily. For some, this could be a relationship breakdown, a change of job, moving house, reaching a salient milestone such as having a significant birthday or simply going on holiday. For example, one woman described how the break-up of her marriage had offered her the opportunity to lose weight:

> I just had to take stock of my life . . . I have gone through a break-up of a marriage, but I have still got two children . . . It's just something inside you that says if you don't sort yourself out. I think losing weight was the hardest and biggest thing that I have achieved.
>
> (Jackie)

For some, it could be feeling breathless when going up stairs or being diagnosed with a health condition. One man described a very serious version of a health crisis:

> I suppose it was like a new life for me . . . when you know you are going to die and when I did get up from the coma. . . . I think it was the first time in my life that I really, really did want to lose the weight. . . .
>
> (Tanvir)

Specific events therefore seem to make it easier to change how we eat and lose weight. In part this is because they can shake up the pattern of our lives. It is also, however, because they offer up an opportunity to reinvent who we are and redefine ourselves in better and healthier ways.

It can't just be the life event itself, however, but the ways in which it makes us think about our lives. For example, one of our participants, Matthew, said this after a heart attack:

> It got to the stage that I knew I was going to die and that was the turning point. I knew I was going to die unless I did something about it. And then I just got into gear and it turned me right around.

But this was after his fourth heart attack aged 37; the first, second and third heart attacks had not had the same impact. Other factors had to have been involved. These are now considered.

Recognising that behaviour is the problem

Many people who are overweight believe in a biological cause of their weight problem, saying, 'It runs in my family', 'I have a slow metabolism', 'I was born like this', 'It's my hormones' or 'My diabetes makes me overweight'. Although there is some evidence that weight is in part influenced by biology and forces beyond our control, this way of thinking does not help us change our behaviour as we believe that there is nothing we can do. For example, if you believe that your heart attack was caused by 'doing too much', you won't follow advice to 'do more exercise' but will prefer to rest and relax. Likewise, if you believe 'I am overweight because of my biology', you won't try to eat less as this doesn't match. Therefore we only adopt solutions to a problem if they match our beliefs about the cause. This is illustrated by one of our participants who had never managed to lose weight and keep it off:

> I was born overweight and I've always been overweight. . . . I was a fat child and then a fat teenager and fat adult and my weight has never decreased, it always just went up. . . . I was never a normal weight.

(Jack)

In contrast, people who have successfully lost weight and kept it off hold a more behavioural model of both the cause of their weight problem, 'I overeat', and the solution, 'I need to eat less'; their model is coherent and emphasises behaviour. For example, as one participant said who has lost and maintained this loss described how his problem had been caused by

> drinking too much . . . eating for comfort . . . lived in a house where there was always much too much to eat . . . finishing off children's food.
>
> (David)

Sometimes this shift towards a behaviour model of body weight may be triggered by the life event itself, or it may come about through something the person has read or seen or as a response to an intervention by a health professional. For example, if someone recognises that they lost weight last time they were ill and gained it whilst on holiday, the link between eating and weight starts to become clearer.

Disrupting the cost-benefit analysis

Most behaviours are governed by a simple cost-benefit analysis, and eating behaviour is no different. Successful weight loss seems to occur when the benefits of the old unhealthy habits no longer outweigh the costs, and at times this can be the result of the life event. For example if someone loses their job, then they no longer get the benefits of eating cakes from the food trolley or having a large pub lunch with colleagues. Similarly, if their marriage breaks up, food need no longer be their way to manage a problematic relationship. The participant who had lost weight described how this had happened after he had split up with his 'monster of a girlfriend':

> Before we split up, I would be happy, then we would have a row or something and I would think, 'Oh, I can't be bothered, I will go out and eat McDonald's'.
>
> (Peter)

But then after we split up, he said,

> I was back home with my family, I was seeing my friends a lot more. . . . I wanted to look good. I wanted to look good naked, that's what I used to say to myself.

The life event had taken away his need to overeat (as he was no longer arguing with his girlfriend) and changed where he lived and who he was living with.

Bringing the costs into the here and now

People are very good at future discounting and will ignore future costs in favour of focusing on any benefits in the here and now. For eating, this can be problematic as the benefits of eating are always immediate whereas the costs are always in the months and years to come. Sometimes life events can change the timing of these costs and benefits by making the costs seem more immediate. For example, if the life event is a health crisis such as a heart attack or a diagnosis of diabetes, then the costs of unhealthy eating are no longer way ahead in the future but have been brought into the here and now, making them harder to ignore. This is also the case with setting achievable goals such as eating regularly or cooking meals rather than snacking. One such goal could be helped by self weighing as this enables the individual to gain regular rewards from sticking to their eating plan. As one of our participants said:

> I go every week to get weighed. Tonight's our night and I'll go tonight to get weighed even though I'm on night shift and I know my weight will be different because I'm on night duty. I will still go and get weighed because I don't want to get out of my target range.
> (Frances)

Successful dieting is therefore not only about disrupting the cost-benefit analysis but also about changing the timing of these factors.

Investment in success

Weight loss can be extremely hard work as it involves changing habits that have been ingrained for a lifetime, existing in a state of denial, missing out on social events and changing the way people live their day-to-day lives. It is sometimes difficult to understand how, when people have been through all this, they put the weight back on, only to have to start the struggle all over again. But fortunately, in many ways, we are not good at remembering difficult episodes in our lives and over time these memories fade, which is helpful for traumatic events but not helpful for dieting as people slip back into their old habits and the weight is regained. Weight loss maintenance seems more likely to occur after initial weight loss if people recognise and can remember how difficult this initial stage was. As one woman said:

> I've worked hard to get it off. . . . I don't want to go back.
>
> (Kerri)

One participant described how she used photos of herself as a means to remember how hard losing weight had been:

> I have pictures of how I used to look stuck up in the bedroom, I've got them stuck on my fridge and inside the cupboard to remind me . . . when I'm thinking oh, I could eat some rubbish, and I am thinking, no. You are not going to start that again.
>
> (Emily)

This is a form of investment that if emphasised, stored, focused on and kept salient can help weight loss maintenance. There are many strategies that can be used to strengthen the sense of investment, such as keeping a diary, filling in a checklist of suffering or writing a list of suffering and placing it in a public place.

A new identity and the process of reinvention

Successful dieters seem to develop a new identity around being a thinner, healthier person, making it harder for them to regain their lost weight as this would no longer be in line with how they see them-selves. For some, this new sense of self can be incorporated into their existing life, but for many it involves a process of reinvention and the establishment of a new way of being which manifests itself in becom-ing something like a gym instructor, a personal trainer, a nutritionist or an organiser for a weight loss group or in taking up triathlons or marathons. Our participants have called this many things, including 'a new start', 'a rebirth', 'a new me' and 'a last chance'. As one man said:

> I feel more confident. . . . I'm less embarrassed and not self con-scious anymore and body language has changed. . . . I can just lean back in my chair and talk. . . . I feel like I've got a new life, new chances, new opportunities. I'm a new person. . . . It is rebirth really.
> (Michael)

And once this new identity has been created, this makes it much more likely that any weight loss will be maintained.

No more emotional eating

Being overweight can often be the response to emotional eating, and food is used to regulate our emotions. As one of our participants said of food:

> I use it so much to control my emotions although of course it never does and makes it worse. It's not a friend but it's an emo-tional support. . . . I have a sort of love/hate relationship with food.
> (Peter)

Successful dieters often talk about finding alternative coping mecha-nisms which can include exercise, talking to friends, singing, playing a musical instrument or finding a new hobby. As one woman said:

> I go and sit in the bath, and I'm learning to deal with my emo-tions differently . . .
> (Krista)

And another said:

> You still do think about it [food], because you don't want to go back where you were, and so you think, what you need to do is occupy your mind, go out for a walk, because when you're out for a walk you can't open the fridge door, so it's a case of occupying your mind.
>
> (Chris)

Finding a substitute coping mechanism isn't easy, though, and several participants have described their struggle to find alternative behaviours:

> If you've used food as your comfort, your security blanket, as your friend, then how do you deal with it if you can't use that anymore? There's no mechanism for me as to how I should deal with things apart from eating.
>
> (Rich)

And for some, their chosen substitute behaviour can also be unhealthy. As one of our patients after bariatric surgery said:

> Post surgery, I definitely transferred to alcohol 'cos I couldn't eat. . . . It was easier and easier to drink to fulfill the need in me.
>
> (Mandi)

A new eating routine

Part of losing weight for the longer term is the establishment of a new healthier routine which can persist for ever onwards rather than just in the shorter term. As one successful dieter described:

> You've got to change your – the way you're eating for a life; it's not just, you know, for a period of time, it's permanent. You've got to make a permanent change, and it's what I've done.
>
> (Mary)

Different success stories involve a wide range of new and different eating habits, and there is no one size of eating habit that fits all.

However, most often when weight loss is maintained, this is associated with eating a healthier diet which is higher in fruit and vegetables and lower in calories. As one woman said:

> I eat more salads, more vegetables, more pickles. . . . I eat plates of boiled vegetables and I eat a lot of salads. I like that. I put horseradish with it sometimes. Sometimes chilli sauce . . . everything I eat now is either brown or natural.
>
> (Jane)

One woman also described how her own healthier eating habits had also influenced the rest of her family:

> We don't go to McDonald's anymore, we don't have pizzas. We used to go to Greggs and buy donuts and we don't do that. . . . Me and my family are being healthy now.
>
> (Angela)

Successful dieting seems to be linked to new habits which can be sustained into the longer term, which also involves changing the habits of others.

Feeling in control

Many people who have lost weight and kept it off describe a new sense of control over food. For those who have used more traditional dieting approaches, this comes from the development of new habits, a reduction in emotional eating due to new alternative coping strategies and a shift in their beliefs about food and the role it plays in their lives. It is also reflected in feeling able to have a level of flexible control rather than seeing food as forbidden or banned:

> We have our little treats, I have had biscuits . . . I don't feel deprived of anything. If I want a chocolate I can have it. You just count it. I can actually still eat quite a lot of the meals I used to eat and I have enjoyed a cooked breakfast this week. The fact that

> I can eat all this, it's tasty and I feel like I am enjoying normal food, not diet food.
>
> (Emily)

Those who had lost weight through obesity surgery also reported a change in control.

For many, this regained sense of control was paradoxically a result of feeling that their choices over food had been taken out of their hands as the operation was limiting their food intake for them. I have called this the 'paradox of control' as by taking away control, surgery can make people feel more in control:

> Now I feel that the control is taken out of my hands. I didn't have that control over my body because my stomach controlled every-thing. If I eat too much I'm sick so I don't have the control any-more . . . that's a good thing because I couldn't control on my own.
>
> (Jenny)

People don't have to have surgery to feel like this. Simply not bringing food into the home can help.

Hope

The final factor that seems to relate to successful weight loss and maintenance is hope. Most people carry on their day to day lives in a habitual way and see their future lives as being very much like the past and present. This is fine for those who are healthy and happy and can lead to contentment and well-being. But for those who are not, it leads to getting stuck. One way to become unstuck is to find a sense of hope that there is another possible future out there which is different and better than the one that has been mapped out for years. For dieters, this sense of hope can come from hearing other people's success stories, taking full credit for times in their own lives when they have changed their behaviour or monitoring their behaviour to find small signs of change to offer hope that change is possible. One of our patients described to us the moment she realised there was hope that her future could be better than her past, and it involved seeing an image of her body during a scan at a hospital:

> My orthopaedic surgeon had a body scan done . . . he said 'there's your body, there's you and there's all your fat . . .' and he said to my kids 'look there's a little Mummy in there trying to get out'. That's when I decided to go for it.
>
> (Rob)

For this woman, the image of the 'little me' version of herself gave her hope which in turn resulted in her changing her behaviour and losing weight.

In-depth accounts of success stories are one approach to discovering the mechanisms behind successful dieting and indicate a number of processes. The second approach to understanding successful dieting is to compare those who have lost weight and kept it off with those who haven't. This will now be considered. Several common elements can be seen across these two approaches.

APPROACH 2: DIFFERENCES BETWEEN THOSE WHO HAVE SHOWN SUCCESSFUL DIETING AND THOSE WHO HAVEN'T

Over the past few decades, several quantitative studies using questionnaires and larger samples have been published exploring the characteristics of those who have managed to lose weight and kept it off versus those who have not. Some of this evidence comes from the National Weight Control Registry (NWCR) in the US which is a database established in 1993 which consists of over 10,000 individuals who have shown more than 30 lbs (13.6 kg) weight loss which has been maintained for more than one year. Although this is not a representative sample as it doesn't include those who have shown no weight loss at all or weight regain within one year, it does provide some useful insights into successful dieting[67-73]. For example, after five years, researchers compared weight loss regainers and maintainers and highlighted key roles for increased physical activity, decreased intake of fat, increased dietary restraint (i.e. dieting efforts), a significant medical trigger and maintaining a consistent diet regimen across the week rather than a more flexible approach to dieting[73].

In a similar vein, I carried out a study in 2000[74] to explore differences between the stable obese, weight loss regainers and weight loss maintainers and identified roles for profile variables, historical factors, help-seeking behaviours and psychological factors. In particular, the weight loss maintainers were older, had dieted for longer, were lighter at the start and reported higher levels of healthy eating (not calorie counting) and showed a lower endorsement of a medical cause of their weight problem, a stronger endorsement of the psychological consequences of being overweight (e.g. body image) and stated that they were motivated to lose weight for psychological reasons (e.g. self esteem and confidence).

A review of the literature exploring successful dieting with a focus on group differences[75] also highlighted a number of strategies associated with success, such as greater initial weight loss, reaching a self determined weight goal, being physically active, eating regular meals throughout the day including breakfast, healthy eating, showing control of overeating, self monitoring of behaviour, being motivated by internal reasons, good coping strategies and a sense of control, autonomy and responsibility.

Finally, a study by myself and my colleague[76] directly tested some of the factors identified by our research on success stories to explore whether the results from these qualitative studies could be supported by quantitative research on a larger sample. The results from this study indicated that those who showed successful dieting and sustained the weight they had lost reported a greater incidence of life events, a belief in the psychological (not medical) solutions to their weight problem and a sense of the new healthier behaviours having more benefits than the older unhealthy behaviours. It seems clear that there are many commonalities between these factors and those illustrated by the qualitative studies exploring success stories.

APPROACH 3: PREDICTING SUCCESSFUL DIETING OVER TIME

The final approach to understanding successful dieting has explored the predictors of weight loss maintenance over time. One study used the NWCR data but with a 10-year follow-up period and found that 87% were still maintaining a loss of at least 10% of their initial body weight by this time[67]. The authors also found that larger weight losses and a longer duration of weight loss maintenance were related to increased physical activity in maintainers' leisure time, higher levels of dietary restraint, increased self weighing, decreased intake of fat and a reduced number of episodes of overeating.

Most other reports, however, have involved synthesis across a number of studies using systematic reviews and meta analyses. For example, Stubbs et al.[77] pooled data across a number of reviews and individual studies of pre-treatment and mid-treatment variables and highlighted that successful dieting was associated with having a higher baseline weight, being male, showing early weight loss when part of an intervention, attendance at the weight loss intervention, increased length of treatment, increased social support, self monitoring of behaviours, goal setting, slowing rate of eating and increased physical activity. Similarly, Teixeira et al.[78] identified factors associated with medium to longer weight control and highlighted the importance of autonomous motivation, self regulation skills, self efficacy, self monitoring and positive body image. Finally, a comprehensive analysis[79] explored the predictors of weight loss by 12 months and reported key roles for calorie counting, greater contact with a dietician and the use of strategies which involved comparison with others.

WHAT COMMON FACTORS RELATE TO SUCCESSFUL DIETING?

Using the three approaches described above, there are clearly a number of overlapping factors that keep reappearing and are linked to successful dieting. I have grouped these together in Table 7.1.

Table 7.1 Understanding successful dieting

Success stories	Differences	Predictors of success	OVERALL THEMES
Life events	Life events, medical triggers		**LIFE EVENTS**
Behavioural model	Reduced medical model		**THINGS CAN CHANGE**
Hope that things can change	Psychological consequences and motivations		
Disrupting costs and benefits of diet and physical activity	New benefits of being healthy	Social comparison Improved body image	**SHIFT IN COST-BENEFIT ANALYSIS**
Changing the timing of costs and benefits	Goal setting, self determined goals	Self weighing, attendance at intervention, goal setting, social support, length of treatment, contact with dietician	
Investment made so far	More dieting attempts, initial weight loss	Early weight loss	**INVESTMENT MADE SO FAR**
New eating regimen	Breakfast, healthy eating, reduced fat, consistent routine	Calorie counting, decreased fat	**NEW BEHAVIOUR REGIMEN**
	Physical activity	Physical activity	
Sense of control	Self monitoring, autonomy, responsibility, increased dieting	Self monitoring, autonomous motivation, increased dieting, decreased overeating, self efficacy	**RENEWED CONTROL**
Less emotional eating	Good coping	Self regulation	
New identity and reinvention			**NEW IDENTITY**

Beyond variables such as being male, being older and having a higher initial body weight, which seem to relate to success but are fixed, this analysis illustrates that there are seven key factors which can be used to explain how some people manage to lose weight and keep it off. First, successful dieting is often **triggered by a life event** or medical trigger which shakes up the person's world and offers a chance for change. If the person also believes in a behavioural model of their weight problem and has hope that **things can change,** this makes initial change more likely. Furthermore, successful dieting is also linked to a **shift in the cost-benefit analysis** of health behaviours, which can be brought around through strategies such as goal setting, self weighing and contact with a formal intervention or dietician which not only enable healthier behaviours to have greater benefits but also bring these benefits into the here and now, making them more sustainable. Next, a successful dieter also seems to need to have made an initial **invest-ment** in change and also to focus on this investment as a way to give momentum to their success, which is illustrated by the effects of early and larger weight loss and the role of simple persistence and repeated attempts at dieting. In turn, this all culminates in a **new consistent behaviour regimen** consisting of breakfast, regular meal times, healthy eating and a reduced intake of fat together with increased physical activity. This is also supported by a **renewed sense of control,** some-times created through self monitoring and illustrated by improved dieting and reduced overeating. Finally, successful dieting also seems to be achieved through the development of a **new identity** and a pro-cess of reinvention, at the centre of which is a healthier, thinner self.

IN SUMMARY

Successful dieting has been explored using three different approaches. Across these different approaches are a number of common factors which seem to facilitate sustained weight loss. These involve an initial trigger, the belief that things can change, a shift in the cost-benefit relationship for eating and exercise, a new behaviour regimen, a sense of control and a new identity. The trick, however, is to make these factors happen rather than just describe them. This is the focus of the final chapters of this book.

8

SOME STRATEGIES
TO CHANGE BEHAVIOUR

Failed dieting is a product of factors that are in our heads, such as emotional triggers, withdrawal, denial and rebound effects, beliefs about food preferences and cross addiction, and aspects of the environment, such as physical triggers and social pressure. Successful dieting seems to be the result of life events, a belief that things can change, a shift in the cost-benefit analysis of eating well, investment in initial weight loss, a sense of renewed control, a new dietary regimen and a new identity as a healthier, thinner person. Bringing about successful weight loss and maintenance is a matter of avoiding those factors that lead to failure and maximising those factors that contribute to success. This involves behaviour change. This chapter will describe some useful strategies that can be used to change behaviour. The following chapter (Chapter 9) will then illustrate how these strategies can be applied to maximise the chances of successful weight loss and maintenance.

UNLEARNING BEHAVIOUR

Any behaviour, whether it be speaking, walking or eating, is learned through the four key mechanisms of modelling (watching others), repetition (doing it over and over), reinforcement (any source of reward) and association (being linked with internal factors such as mood or external factors in our environment). Changing behaviour therefore involves unlearning the old behaviour and learning the new behaviour using these same mechanisms in the following ways:

Modelling: We can change our behaviour by watching those around us and focusing on the behaviours we want to copy. This could be the behaviour of our family, friends, health care professionals, teachers, work colleagues or even people we see from a distance via the media in magazines or on the TV. Therefore, if you want to change your behaviour, it is helpful to surround yourself with people who behave in the desired way, to make yourself attend to those who behave more healthily and to try to discount those that do not. This is known as modelling, observational learning or social learning.

Repetition: The best predictor of future behaviour is past behaviour as we are creatures of habit[60,61]. But the difficult stage is often to get a behaviour to become a habit in the first place. Therefore, rather on relying on the more unconscious processes of a habit at the beginning of behaviour change, it is necessary just to keep repeating a behaviour over and over so that it starts to feel more normal. This can be facilitated by using the mechanisms of reinforcement and association.

Reinforcement: A behaviour is always more likely to reoccur if it is reinforced or rewarded in some way. This can be through someone else smiling, praising you or showing pleasure, through self reward in the form of stickers on a sticker chart, treats, gaining or saving money or just self praise. But however it comes, praise will help to make a new behaviour happen again. And positive reinforcement is always far more effective than criticism, which can often just lower people's self esteem or mood rather than change their behaviour.

Association: Any behaviour will become associated with internal factors such as mood or external aspects of the environment. Changing behaviour therefore involves making new associations so that the newer, healthier behaviour becomes more positive and the older, unhealthier behaviour becomes more negative. This can be achieved through searching for images of disease and placing them next to images of unhealthy foods; finding images of a healthy life and placing them next to images of healthier foods; making yourself associate fast food restaurants with feelings of over fullness, tiredness, nausea and poor taste; learning to associate eating well with feelings of health and well-being; and pairing the feelings of being outside in fresh air and doing exercise with renewed energy.

The mechanisms of modelling, repetition, reinforcement and association can therefore be used to unlearn a behaviour. For successful dieting, this could involve making sure you spend more time with those who eat well and exercise and attend to those around you who have healthier habits (rather than focusing on those who do not); forcing yourself at first to start a new eating habit and then repeating it over and over, even if you don't want to; rewarding yourself wherever possible for anything you do that is healthier, whether it be just trying harder, thinking about eating well or actually eating well; and being more active and then trying to make positive associations between your new eating habits and positive ideas such as health, happiness, living longer, not being ill and having fun.

CHANGING COGNITIONS

Behaviour is not only driven by the mechanisms described above but also by cognitions which can also be changed. For example, we might eat fast foods because we think, 'Cooking takes time' or 'Cooking is so complicated these days, I'll never be like one of those chefs on the TV', and we might overeat because we think, 'My life is so stressful, eating is the only way I know how to make myself feel better'. Research shows that cognitions can be changed through the use of 'Socratic questions' which involve searching for evidence to see whether any given cognition is actually backed up by anything. For example, if someone says, 'Nobody likes me', then you search to find evidence of people who do like them; if they say, 'I always fail', then you search for evidence to show that sometimes they succeed; and if they say, 'If I can't be the best then I'm useless', you find evidence when they were good enough and this was fine. These Socratic questions form the basis of a process called cognitive restructuring and this, together with the mechanisms of unlearning behaviour, is the essence of Cognitive Behavioural Therapy (CBT), which is used in a multitude of settings and is an effective way to change behaviour[80].

One additional approach that can be used to change behaviour draws upon the basics of CBT and is called Relapse Prevention; it has mostly been used to change addictive behaviours. Relapse Prevention involves a multitude of strategies including relaxation, contract setting and skills training but the concept which is of most relevance to dieting is the Abstinence Violation Effect[81]. This effect describes the stage between an initial lapse (i.e. eating one biscuit) and a full-blown relapse (i.e. eating the whole packet) and offers an analysis of how to make a relapse less likely. Specifically, the approach argues that a lapse turns into a relapse if the individual blames themselves and experiences a sense of cognitive dissonance due to the uncomfortable gap between how they see themselves (i.e. as someone who is dieting) versus their actual behaviour (i.e. as someone who has just lapsed). It then argues that the best intervention is to encourage people to find something else to blame other than themselves, such as the situation (i.e. 'I was at a party', 'Someone offered me it', 'I had had a difficult day'). That way, the person doesn't experience self blame, their dissonance is reduced and they can return to their diet and avoid the relapse. This process finds parallels in the notion of the 'what the hell' effect in the dieting literature and is a useful approach to behaviour change.

SENSE MAKING

Life is full of both positive and negative events, yet how we feel about our lives often relates to how we make sense of our world rather than what is objectively happening to us. Further, we find it hard to live with uncertainty and chance and so search for patterns in what we see, do and experience. This results in a process of sense making which is central to our health as it influences the stories we tell ourselves about what we do ('I eat to cheer myself up'), who we are ('I am lazy') and where we come from ('I am just like my parents'). Sense making is central to behaviour change in two ways.

First, we tend to develop coherent stories about the cause and solution to any given problem. So if we believe 'I am overweight because of my hormones', then we will also believe 'I need a drug to help me lose weight – there is nothing I can do'. Changing our behaviour would not make sense within this model of our health. Likewise, if we believe 'My knees hurt because I am doing too much', then the obvious solution is to do less and avoid the cause of the pain. However, if we believe 'I am overweight because I eat too much' or 'My knees hurt because I don't do enough exercise', eating less and doing more would seem to be the perfect solutions. This need for coherence therefore determines which solutions people are more or less likely to adopt[82]. Behaviour change requires a shift towards beliefs about causes which include behaviour as a means to encourage the uptake of behavioural solutions. This can be achieved using CBT as described above.

Second, we also develop stories about how we are feeling and are often driven to re-establish the status quo after any change so that we can feel fine again. For example, if something goes wrong in our lives such as a relationship breakdown, a diagnosis or the loss of a job, we feel unsettled. As a result, we tell ourselves the story that this was a blip in our lives and that everything will be better once we have got back to where we were before this happened so we can start to feel normal again. This urge to re-establish equilibrium is a powerful coping mechanism and helps to maintain a sense of stability[83]. At times, however, this drive can be harmful if it means that we miss an opportunity for change. In terms of behaviour, shifts in the status quo can offer a chance for change, but they need to be embraced and seen as an opportunity rather than a threat and the temptation to return to how we were before needs to be overcome. This can also be achieved through CBT and attempts to change the ways in which a person makes sense of their world.

MAKING PLANS

One of the simplest ways to promote behaviour change is to set goals and make plans. These should be clear and specific, describing the what, where and when of any given behaviour. In psychology these are sometimes referred to as 'implementation intentions' and refer to goals such as 'I will eat fish and rice for lunch at 12.00 tomorrow' rather than 'I will eat more healthily'. In the broader health literature the best goals are said to be SMART: Specific, Measurable, Attainable, Relevant and Timely. Research indicates that goal setting can help to change a range of health-related behaviours[84]. They can be made even more effective if these goals are shared with others and made public. This can form the basis of a psychological contract between a person and their family or friends or health care professional, which then makes the goals harder to break.

INCREASING MOTIVATION

Health care professionals often use the stages of change model to describe how ready their clients are to change. This model describes five different stages: pre-contemplation (not thinking about change), contemplation (thinking about change), preparation (starting to prepare for change), action (making changes), maintenance (keeping the changes) then relapse (going back to the old behaviour)[85]. Although this model has been criticised in many ways, it is a useful way of describing people at the start of any behaviour change intervention and has led to two key developments for behaviour change. The first is the notion of a stage-matched intervention, which simply states that any intervention should be matched to the person's readiness to change. Therefore, if someone is still in the pre-contemplation stage, it is probably not worth trying to get them to change yet. Second, the stages of change approach has resulted in the development of motivational interviewing, which is very commonly used to change behaviour and move people between stages[86]. Motivational interviewing focuses on the notion of cognitive dissonance, which is the uncomfortable feeling people get when there is a mismatch between how they see themselves and how they are behaving[87]. For example, if you see yourself as kind but have just been mean, you will experience a sense of cognitive dissonance. Similarly, if you think 'I am a sensible person who takes care of myself' but also 'I eat too much and am making myself ill', you will likewise feel dissonance. Some therapies try to make the dissonance go away using reassurance. Motivational interviewing does the opposite and tries to make the dissonance worse based upon the premise that this increased dissonance will push people to change what they do. This is achieved by asking people to describe the costs and benefits of their behaviour, then feeding these back to them so that they can see the gap between one set of beliefs about themselves and what they are doing. So if you are overweight, you might think 'I like eating a lot as it helps me manage my emotions' and also think 'My weight is making me miserable'. If these mismatching thoughts are then fed back to you, you should then think 'Time to change how I eat'.

Motivational interviewing can be used by health care professionals to change the behaviour of others. But it can also be used to promote self change, particularly if you write down the different costs and benefits and then make yourself compare and contrast and expose the dissonance.

USING EMOTION

For many years, health promotion campaigners believed that fear was the best strategy to change behaviour, and as a result, smoking cessation campaigns included phrases such as 'Smoking kills' or 'Smoking seriously damages your health'. This approach was informed by the notion of a fear appeal, whereby campaigns were designed to make people frightened. For weight loss, such a fear appeal first emphasised health problems: 'There is a threat by being overweight', naming heart disease and diabetes. It also told people 'You are at risk' – 'Being overweight puts you at risk of a heart attack' – and 'The threat is serious: heart attacks kill'. This was then followed by a safety condition which explained how people could avoid this threat: 'a recommended protective action' would be 'eat less', 'do more exercise'. People were also told 'The action is effective' – 'eating a healthy diet helps protect against having a heart attack' – and 'The action is easy: healthy eating is easy and cheap'. Unfortunately, evidence indicated that these fear appeals were not very effective and that either too much or too little fear caused people to ignore this information[88]. In particular, it seems that when frightened, people block such messages as they create a dissonance between how they see themselves and how they are behaving, which challenges their sense of integrity. This blocking is achieved by a number of methods including denigrating the message ('It's not very clear', 'The leaflet is badly designed') and questioning its source ('Scientists can't be trusted') or the messenger ('You're fat, what do you know about weight loss' or 'You're thin, what do you know about weight loss').

There are three possible solutions to the problem of blocking. The first is simply to identify the perfect 'moderate' amount of fear and use this. This is difficult, however, as each individual has their own fear response and so judging the level of fear necessary either at a population or individual level would be pretty much impossible. The second approach is to use images rather than just text. Much research indicates that visual imagery is harder to block than text alone as it seems to directly influence our emotions whilst bypassing our cognitions so that we are unable to 'intellectually' rationalise and dismiss the messages they present[89]. Finally, there is also evidence that negative messages may be more likely to be heard if the person is helped to feel good about themselves beforehand. This can be achieved through either self affirmation or encouraging gratitude. Self affirmation is a process by which a person is asked to consider good things about themselves. This could be 'Think of 10 times when you have been kind' or 'Write down 10 things that you are good at'. Likewise, gratitude interventions encourage people to focus on the good things in their life that they can feel grateful for (e.g. 'I have nice parents', 'My job is secure', 'My children are well'). Once self affirmed or feeling more grateful, people feel better about themselves and therefore less threatened by messages telling them that how they behave should change[90]. This is similar to the notion of a 'feedback sandwich' in education (i.e. 'Well done for answering the question, but you could have added more evidence'), the recommended mode of communication for a medical consultation (i.e. 'The good news is this, but the bad news is that') and the counselling approach to managing conflict in relationships (i.e. 'Thanks for doing the washing up, but it would help if you cooked sometimes').

Emotions can therefore be used to change behaviour, but on their own fear appeals do not appear to be very effective as people block them. This can be solved by pitching fear at the right level or using imagery, self affirmation and gratitude. Such strategies can be used for successful dieting both by dieters themselves and by health care professionals helping others to lose weight.

SELF MONITORING

Habits are often embedded and therefore occur with very little conscious thought. This is why we can drive along familiar routes without really noticing where we are and eat our way through a loaf of bread or bag of chips without registering whether or not we are still hungry. One strategy to prevent such mindless behaviour and to make it more mindful is to self monitor, making our behaviour more conscious and less automatic. This can be achieved by making plans as described above. But it can also be helped by simple tricks such as taking a shopping list to the supermarket, eating at a table with a plate and knife and fork or going to a club once a week to be weighed. Self monitoring can be problematic in life if it results in people becoming overly inwardly focused as they can become too concerned about their bodily symptoms and health. But when trying to change a habit, self monitoring can help to create an initial change in behaviour and then help prevent a slip back into old ways until the new habit has been established.

IN SUMMARY

Habits are difficult to change as they have often been entrenched from childhood and are responses to what's in our heads and the triggers in our environment. This chapter has outlined some useful behaviour change strategies that can be used to facilitate changes both in eating and exercise behaviours, including unlearning behaviours, changing cognitions, sense making, making plans, improving motivation, using emotion and self monitoring. The next chapter will illustrate how these strategies can be directly applied to successful dieting in a tool kit for dieting well.

9

A TOOL KIT FOR DIETING WELL
Making successful dieting happen

This chapter will pull together the literature on failed and successful dieting with a range of behaviour change strategies to describe the best approach to dieting well. We therefore need to change how we think and what we do in ways that are sustainable for the rest of our lives, making success much more likely whilst avoiding the pitfalls that lead to failure. Ultimately this all involves building new healthy habits which will eventually become as difficult to change as the unhealthy ones were. I think this can be achieved through a five-step approach, as illustrated in Table 9.1.

STEP 1: FINDING THE TRIGGER TO CHANGE

Successful weight loss and maintenance is often triggered by a life event. Yet we can't make life events happen, which is problematic if we are to try and promote successful dieting. But very often in our day to day lives, there are mini life events such as aches and pains, a change in what we can and cannot do, a birthday or special celebration, a change of location or routine brought about by a holiday, a new job or new house, a comment from others or even just a change in the lives of those around us. And these all offer up the potential for change. The tendency is to let these moments pass

Table 9.1 A tool kit for dieting well: a five-step approach

Successful dieting	5 steps to dieting well	A tool kit of strategies
LIFE EVENTS	1 **Finding the trigger to change**	Reframing threat as opportunity
THINGS CAN CHANGE **SHIFT IN COST-BENEFIT ANALYSIS** **INVESTMENT MADE SO FAR**	2 **Changing what's in our heads**	Cognitive restructuring Searching for evidence Reframing stories about cause and solutions Finding new role models Focusing on stories of hope Reinforcement Associations Using imagery Self monitoring Making plans Setting achievable goals Focusing on symptoms now
NEW BEHAVIOUR REGIMEN	3 **Creating a new behaviour regimen**	Modelling Repetition Reinforcement Associations Planning Self monitoring Reframing food as meals, not snacks Using imagery
	4 **Managing the environment**	Planning Self monitoring Avoidance
RENEWED CONTROL **NEW IDENTITY**	5 **Paving the way forward**	Self monitoring Mindful behaviour External blame Self compassion Reframing failure as an opportunity for change

you by and to re-establish a sense of normality by settling back into your normal way of thinking. But the trick is to identify one of these changes in your life as a potential life event, think about it, focus on it, write about it or tell others about it and use this as an opportunity for change. In medicine these are called 'teachable moments', and doctors can use them to get the message across to patients that something needs to change. In life we can create our own teachable moments by focusing on any opportunity for change and making it the trigger that we need to make things different in the future. This can be achieved through understanding the importance of sense making and seeing any event that disrupts the routines of our lives as an opportunity, not a threat.

STEP 2: CHANGING WHAT'S IN OUR HEADS

The way in which you think can help your diet either fail or succeed. In order for weight to be lost and maintained, you need to first believe that things can change, then shift the cost-benefit analysis of a healthier lifestyle and finally focus on any investment you have made in the initial stages of losing weight. These can be achieved by doing the following.

Believing things can change

Many people turn to biological models of their weight and believe 'It runs in my family', 'It's genetic', 'It's caused by my diabetes' or 'It's my hormones'. All of these models can generate feelings of hopelessness and powerlessness which result in doing nothing. Whether there is any truth in any of these beliefs doesn't really matter, but if a person wants to lose weight, then they have to believe that they can; to do this, they have to believe that their weight is a product of what they do and that what they do can change. And this can be achieved through cognitive restructuring and the use of CBT or through searching for new role models.

People can also use CBT on themselves. So if you think 'My weight is due to my genetics and there is nothing I can do about it', ask yourself, 'Has my weight ever gone down?' and 'Has my weight ever gone up?' If the answer is 'Last year I put on weight during my holiday in Spain' and 'I lost weight after I had flu', next, think, 'Why was this?' The answer may well be 'I put on weight in Spain because we went out for dinner every night and the food was amazing' and 'I lost weight when I had flu as I was in bed for a week and just lost my appetite'. It then starts to become clear that body weight is linked to behaviour and that eating more results in weight gain and eating less leads to weight loss. If you then search for more evidence that behaviour is linked to changes in weight, you may well find several other examples, such as 'During pregnancy I needed to eat more as I was starving all the time' or 'When I started my new job I put on weight as they had a cake trolley' or 'I lost weight for our holiday last year by cutting down on snacks but put it back on whilst we were away as the hotel gave us cooked breakfasts every day'. Eventually it becomes obvious that weight can change and that this change can be brought about through behaviour. And once you believe this, you will feel less powerless and hopeless over your weight and more likely to succeed in making a difference.

Believing that things can change can also be achieved by searching for new role models that can offer hope of a new future. The media surrounds us with images and stories of a wide range of people, and in our own lives we see, know or hear of those who manage their lives in different ways. Some of these people may illustrate how hard it is to change, and in terms of weight loss, there are endless examples of failed dieting and weight regain. But there are also success stories out there that can be an inspiration and offer hope that change is possible. The trick is to focus on these more hopeful stories, to make these people your role models, to learn about them, watch them and talk about them, and then through modelling and a renewed sense of hope, this will help to generate a sense that success is actually possible.

Shifting the cost-benefit analysis

At its simplest, we carry out any behaviour because at the time, the benefits of this behaviour outweigh the costs. Successful dieting requires two key changes. The first is to the cost-benefit analysis itself, and the second is to the timing of this analysis.

The cost-benefit analysis itself

Successful dieting for the longer term requires a shift in the cost-benefit analysis to not only make the benefits of eating well (and less) outweigh the benefits of not eating well (or eating more) but also make the costs of not eating well outweigh the benefits of not eating well! (And the same for physical activity!) **The benefits of eating well** can be increased by strategies such as setting up a rewards system and a process of reinforcement for a wide range of outcomes. To this end, set up a series of detailed, achievable goals for a wide range of behaviours related to weight change, including effort (trying to eat well, trying to exercise, remembering to try, turning up for support groups, seeking help from friends and family), shopping behaviour (planning meals, buying ingredients, shopping for healthier items), cooking behaviour (cooking more from scratch, eating in, not eating ready meals or takeaways, cooking meals), eating behaviour (cooking healthier meals, eating more fruit and vegetables, eating less fat, not snacking, eating breakfast), change in body weight (self weighing, weight loss) and state of mind (positive mood, setting up achievable goals not only for body weight, motivation, body image, self esteem). Then, on a regular basis, when *any* of these goals has been met, you need to be rewarded using any kind of reinforcement that works for you. This can be a sticker on a sticker chart on the fridge, money or pasta pieces in a jar, a smiley face or a tick on a list or a call to a friend to tell them how well you are doing. Then, when there are enough stickers, money, pasta pieces, ticks, smiley faces or calls, this needs to be rewarded even more using something 'better', such as a hot bath, a trip to the shops or a night out. Similarly, you can get help from a dietician, counsellor, nutritionist or weight management group leader or from other people trying to lose weight as a way to gain reinforcement for your behaviour. This way 'good behaviour' is being reinforced, the benefits of eating well are increasing, and if there are enough goals, then there will always be something to reward.

Similarly, the **benefits of being more active** can also be increased by setting up a wide range of goals (use the stairs, walk up the escalators, walk to work, go for a walk, go to the gym, go for a run, play sport) which can also be reinforced once these goals have been met. We are all hugely motivated by positive reinforcement rather than criticism. It is therefore a more powerful incentive to set goals and meet them than it is to fail. So by setting a range of goals, it is more likely that some will gain a reward, making it more likely that the behaviour will carry on.

A shift in this cost-benefit analysis also involves highlighting the **costs of not eating well** so that these are easier to be outweighed by the benefits. In the main these costs are in the future, which can make them easy to ignore (see below), but there are some strategies to make them seem more salient. One key way is to use your emotions and to see the potential consequences of being overweight as unpleasant, damaging or even frightening. This can be achieved through searching out images of body fat and how it surrounds and suffocates our organs or pictures of arteries being blocked and the damage this does to our heart; reading about the hormones produced by body fat and how these generate hormones which make us more susceptible to cancer and diabetes as they flood our womb with oestrogen or stop the pancreas from working efficiently; or looking at websites on joint trauma and how every step up stairs places 10 times the weight of the body on our knees, causing knee pain and ultimately decaying the knee joint. Such images can trigger an emotional reaction which may help to shift the cost-benefit analysis and change behaviour. Likewise, by emphasising the costs of unhealthy behaviour, this can generate a sense of dissonance, which is uncomfortable and can prompt a desire to change in order to remove the dissonance. Too much negative emotion, however, can push people into denial, leading to them blocking what they don't want to know. To avoid this happening, it helps to do something first to make you feel good about yourself. This could be a self affirmation intervention (reflect on 10 things about yourself which are good) or a gratitude intervention (write down 10 things in your life that you are grateful for). That way, when you search out emotional information, you may be more able to process it in a more constructive way.

The timing of the cost-benefit analysis

Very often the costs of behaving in an unhealthy way are far off in the future and can be discounted as they are outweighed by the more immediate benefits. Successful dieting requires the **timing of the costs** of not eating well to be brought into the here and now. This can be done in a number of ways. For example, the meaning of different foods can be changed so that unhealthy foods start to become aversive and unpleasant rather than appealing. This can be achieved by changing what associations you have with different foods through the use of images of heart disease, body fat around the organs, cancers or amputations from diabetes, which will make the consequences of poor health seem more immediate. It also helps to focus on current physical symptoms you may have: breathlessness; joint pain in the knees, hips or back; difficulty in getting up from the floor, going up stairs or running to catch a bus. Although it may be easy to discount a heart attack in 20 years' time, it becomes harder to discount if the symptoms are happening now. Images of what is in certain meals could also help, such as the amount of sugar in fizzy drinks and fast food, the level of fat in takeaways or the number of additives in ready meals. This information can be found using specific apps on your phone or through searching the internet and will help shift beliefs about the costs of unhealthy behaviour. Further, it can help to focus on the ill health of others, either in real life or on the TV or radio, and consider how their health problems have been a product of their behaviour. This was particularly apparent in 2016 with the high number of deaths of rock and roll celebrities, many of whom had lived unhealthy lifestyles. In the same way that positive role models can help to create a sense that things can change, focusing on others who have not fared so well can help to make the longer term consequences of being overweight seem more real again making them more difficult to discount.

Focusing on investment

Evidence indicates that up to about 60% of people manage to lose weight in the first instance using a wide range of weight control strategies[37]. This initial stage can involve a huge amount of effort as it requires changing behaviours which are often embedded from childhood and learning to eat in new and different ways. Research suggests that one of the key ways that this initial weight loss can be translated into longer term weight loss maintenance is through focusing on the investment required in this initial weight loss stage. We know from research on placebos that the more effort an intervention requires (e.g. a more complicated trip to a faith healer, a larger pill, surgery, paying more money, spending more time), the more effective the intervention is. We also know that those who show successful dieting are more aware of the investment they have made. Therefore, the third way that we need to change what's in our heads is to increase a sense that the initial weight loss required a greater degree of investment[91]. This could be achieved through self monitoring by keeping a diary of the efforts made and the struggles involved, using photos to remind you of any difficult days and how you survived them, telling others how difficult it has been and getting them to remind you on a regular basis or simply making a list of all the difficult aspects of losing weight, putting the list on the fridge and reading it regularly to remind yourself.

The second step to dieting well therefore involves changing what is inside your head in terms of believing that things can change, shifting the cost-benefit analysis and focusing on the investment needed to generate any initial weight loss in the first place. And these changes can be achieved by applying a wide range of behaviour change strategies such as reinforcement, modelling, cognitive restructuring, images, cognitive dissonance, self monitoring and planning.

STEP 3: CREATING A NEW BEHAVIOUR REGIMEN

Research exploring failed and successful dieting indicates that a new behaviour regimen is necessary if you are to lose weight and keep it off in the longer term. This new regimen can be understood in terms of what, where, when and why to eat, as follows.

What to eat

The media would have us believe that nutritional recommendations for a healthy diet are forever changing and that we cannot trust what we are told. Although there are ongoing debates about the detail, in the main the notion of a healthy diet has been fairly consistent for about the past 30 years. It consists of a high level of fruit and vegetables; a high level of whole-grain complex carbohydrates such as brown rice, brown pasta and brown bread; medium amounts of protein in the form of meat, fish or pulses; low levels of fat and very low levels of foods with added sugars, such as cakes, chocolate and sweets. This is what should be consumed by those wishing to maintain a healthy body weight and aiming to avoid all the ill health consequences of a poor diet. In terms of losing weight, the same goal of healthy eating still applies, but in addition, the amount of energy consumed needs to be less than the amount of energy being used up by day to day living. This mostly involves eating less and can be achieved in a vast array of different ways that can be found in all the hundreds of dieting books in the bookshops. But the evidence indicates that the most effective way to eat less overall and to sustain this over the longer term is to reduce your fat intake by eating more fruit and vegetables, by watching (and maybe counting) your calorie intake, by eating a healthy and balanced diet, by having a consistent routine that spreads across all seven days of the week, by becoming more physically active and by eating breakfast each day (although there is some evidence that missing breakfast can also sometimes help as long as people can make it to lunch without compensating midmorning)[92]. At its simplest, to lose weight you need to eat less than you usually eat. The evidence points to some ways that this can be achieved, but basically people have to find the way that best fits with their lifestyle and individual needs – there is no miracle one-size-fits-all approach. But managing where, when and how you eat will definitely help.

Where to eat

The modern world makes it easy to overeat without realising as we grab food 'on the go' in between meetings or in the car, wolf down food whilst still sitting at our desk or eat in the evenings whilst watching TV. As a result, much of this eating is done mindlessly and without thinking, and this means we don't process our eating behaviour and so don't feel as full afterwards. We have carried out a series of studies on the impact of the place of eating on food intake and found that people eat more when distracted in front of the TV, that they eat more later on if they have eaten a snack whilst walking around corridors and that they eat less later on if they sit in a chair and eat at a table with a plate, knife and fork than if they stand up and eat from a snack box with a plastic fork[93]. In fact we even found that they eat more later on if the food they have eaten is called a 'snack' rather than a 'meal', even when it is exactly the same amount of food! It would therefore seem best to eat at a table so that you can eat more mindfully and call it a 'meal' whilst doing so. In turn this helps to limit emotional eating and also enables you to self monitor what you are doing.

When to eat

We eat for so many reasons other than hunger, including feeling bored, being in need of a treat, for comfort or because others are eating. This again can all lead to overeating. Ideally, in order to eat less, we therefore need to try and work out when we are actually hungry and only eat then, yet this is difficult given the many roles that food now has in our lives. One way to help this process is to eat at specified times of the day and to plan when and what each meal is going to be. This helps in several ways. First, it is a basic form of goal setting and helps change behaviour. Second, it involves self monitoring, which undermines mindless eating and encourages less distraction. Third, it avoids snacking often prompted by triggers in the environment. Finally, it helps you to learn to accept the feeling of hunger that develops in between eating, to welcome this feeling rather than fear it and to learn that a meal is far more rewarding if you are hungry when you eat it.

Why to eat

We should therefore plan what to eat, change where we eat and sit at a table, call this a meal and eat at specified times which have been planned and can be anticipated. In turn this will inevitably change why we eat as we will no longer be able to spontaneously eat in response to the things inside our heads or the triggers in our environment. Paradoxically, although this all involves greater thought and organisation in the first instance, ultimately it will enable food to become less of a focus in our lives and we can live to eat, not eat to live.

This third step to dieting well involves establishing a new eating regimen that in turn can become a new habit and carry us through into our future lives. This requires a change in what, where, when and why we eat. This involves a range of strategies including planning and self monitoring so as to eat in a more mindful way and reframing food as meals not snacks.

STEP 4: MANAGING THE ENVIRONMENT

Our behaviour is clearly a response to what's in our heads and the triggers in our environment. Ideally we would all be able to re-programme what's in our heads so that we can ignore these external triggers and just do what, where, when and why we plan to do, as described above. But this can be hard at times, and extra help is needed in the form of managing both the home environment and the world out there.

The home environment

As adults, we are in charge of our home environment. We have the car and the money, we do the shopping and the cooking, we buy the furniture and decide how the day should be structured. We therefore need to manage our homes in such a way as to make it as easy as possible to eat what, when, where and why we plan to. This can be achieved in a number of ways but which mostly involve lists, plans, self monitoring, goals and routine! First, only food that you plan to eat should be brought into the house. If you don't want to eat it, then don't buy it. So plan your meals for the week, write a list of ingredients for these meals (not snacks), buy these ingredients (only) and bring them home. This can be helped by shopping when full, by not going down the supermarket aisles that sell fizzy drinks, sweets, chocolates or cakes, and by not taking small children food shopping if you can help it. Second, you need to choose a place to eat. Ideally this should be at a make it harder to then eat high front of the TV or computer. Over time, this place needs to become associated with eating so that eating anywhere else will feel strange. This will happen through simple repetition which will gradually normalise the idea of only eating at the table. Third, you then need to choose when to eat. Obviously our modern lives are busy, complicated and often chaotic, particularly if lots of other people are involved. But, if possible, plan to eat three times a day, for breakfast, lunch and dinner. Plan to eat dinner early rather than later (late evening eating causes more fat to be laid down and can disturb sleep), and eat these meals at a table and tell yourself you are having 'a meal'. Try to stick to this as much as possible. Learn that the feeling of hunger you get as meal time approaches is a good feeling as you enjoy your meal more, and learn that this feeling goes away once you have eaten. Soon, eating at other times of day will start to feel strange as these planned meal times become the new normal. Finally, as part of changing what you eat, you need to eat more fruit and vegetables as these are not only healthy but also stop you feeling hungry and make it harder to then eat high fat, high calorie meals or snacks. So you need to buy more fruits and vegetables and bring them into the house, but then in order for you to eat them, they need to be accessible. Although snacking traditional snacks of crisps and biscuits is not a good idea, mindlessly reaching for some grapes or an apple is a good way to achieve the recommended five servings a day. So buy a fruit bowl, fill it with fruit and place it on a table in easy reach.

For some people, however, the home environment may not seem so controllable if they are not the one who manages the shopping and cooking or if they have to cook for others who have their own views about what and when food should be eaten. This can be problematic. Some possible solutions to this involve encouraging others to see the benefits of eating well and the costs of not eating well, rewarding them for supporting you using praise and smiles, offering to help in other ways if they can change how they cook, offering to take on some of the cooking and shopping, and helping them to see how important it is to eat well by using all the techniques described above.

The world out there

The world out there is much harder to manage than our own home environment, and the danger zones in this outside world vary hugely according to where we live, work, shop and socialise and how we live our lives. But there are still several strategies that can limit the ways in which this world tricks us into eating more and doing less. Again, this mostly requires plans, goals, self monitoring and routine along with a good dose of avoidance. For example, some restaurants sell high fat, high calorie fast food meals and encourage eating on the go. So don't go there. That way, you won't be tempted. Some work places have cake trolleys, biscuit tins and huge boxes of sweets whenever there is something to celebrate. I would recommend suggesting these are stopped, and if this fails, you could find a route around the office that avoids going near them or you could get them placed in a more tucked-away location. Most restaurants offer a wide range of meals from the simple and unfulfilling side salad to the most indulgent gourmet meal. And when we are at a table surrounded by friends, with peer pressure at its peak, our decisions tend to be governed by those around us. But if you can see the menu beforehand, have time and space to plan and then know what you have already chosen, you can select something that you like and that will fill you up but that fits in with your daily routine rather than giving into impulse buys or choices driven by the choices of others. Finally, supermarkets can also be problematic with their aisles of fizzy drinks, sweets and biscuits and fresh-smelling bakeries with their newly baked cakes. But this can also be managed by writing a detailed shopping list (of ingredients for meals, not snacks), avoiding the danger zones and not shopping when hungry.

The fourth step to dieting well therefore involves managing the environment both in the home and out there in the world. Ideally, we would all have cognitive strategies to help us deal with these triggers, but sometimes it is just easier (and more effective) to avoid them.

STEP 5: PAVING THE WAY FORWARD

The final step to successful and sustained weight loss involves paving the way forward towards a renewed sense of control and ultimately a new identity as a thinner, healthier person. This involves carrying on with all the steps described above. It also involves coping with failure and a process of reinvention.

Coping with failure

However determined, organised or motivated you are and however much you try to follow each and every strategy suggested in this book, there will always be times when you will eat more than you would like, miss a session at the gym and see the scales start to slip back up. The trick is not to kid yourself that these moments won't happen but to have a set of strategies ready for when they inevitably do. That way a lapse won't turn into a full-blown relapse, the 'what the hell' effect can be avoided and your self esteem can remain intact. Here are some strategies that should work.

Plan how to deal with a high risk situation

There will always be times and places that are harder to manage, such as a dinner party, a special celebration, a holiday or when you are tired or feeling down. One way to manage these is to imagine beforehand what these situations might be, put yourself into the situation and consider how you will feel. Then plan what you will do and say. That way, when these things happen, you will be better prepared and less likely to resort to an automatic slip back into old habits.

Blame the situation, not yourself

At times this won't work and you will overeat or not be as active as you would like. Blaming yourself is the most common reaction, which can lead to negative mood and lowered self esteem, which in turn can easily result in further eating and then the downward spiral continues. The better solution is to find something else to blame: other people who cooked you the food, the fact that it was a wedding, work stress that made you need to eat, the fact that you needed the holiday. That way you can keep your self esteem intact and resolve to start again immediately.

Be kind to yourself

Self compassion and self forgiveness are key if changes are to be sustained for the longer term[94]. It is important to work on the way that you think and manage your environment, but when this doesn't work, it is also important to be kind to yourself as that way your self esteem can stay intact and you are more likely to be successful in the longer term. Some researchers have coined the term *self licensing* to describe the ways in which people justify their daily slips in behaviour by saying 'Just this once', or 'It won't do any harm', or 'I'll be back on track tomorrow'. This level of being kind isn't helpful as it prevents you from meeting any of the goals you have set. But the aim is to try hard all the time, stick to your plans most of the time and then on the odd occasion when you don't, forgive yourself, understand why it happened and then move on.

See it as a learning opportunity, not a failure

Part of self compassion is the way in which you frame failure, and central to this is the process of sense making. In fact the word *failure* is itself problematic as this is harsh and critical and would be better off framed as a learning opportunity. Therefore, when you haven't managed to behave as you would have wished to, critically evaluate the situation which led to this slip, understand what was happening in the world around you, reflect on how you were feeling and what you were thinking and work out how you can manage this situation better in the future.

Remember all your achievements so far

Finally, try to remember all that you have achieved so far in terms of what is going on in your head, the way you think and feel about food, your attempts and successes at eating less and doing more and any weight you have lost. Focusing on these achievements will enable you to maximise the investment you have made in successful dieting, which will give you the momentum to keep going. It will also help maintain your confidence at your abilities to change. The first stage of paving the way forward therefore involves learning to manage failure in a positive and constructive way in order to see it as a learning opportunity in the context of all that you have achieved so far. The final step is the process of reinvention which is key to creating a new identity.

The process of reinvention

Even when they have lost weight, people often describe how they still see themselves as overweight, how they wander into outsize clothes shops, how they take larger clothes into the changing rooms and how they are constantly surprised when these clothes don't fit or when they see their thinner selves in a shop window. They also comment that it takes a while for their new confidence to develop and that the 'ghost' of their older self takes time to fall away. Yet evidence indicates that successful dieting which lasts into the longer term is associated with a process of reinvention and the creating of a new identity as a thinner, more active and healthier person. This is probably because it is much easier to slip back into old ways and regain any weight lost if you still see yourself as that heavier person. So how does reinvention occur?

Investment

First, it is key to focus on all the efforts you have made to get this far. We know that any intervention is more effective if it involves more effort, and given that weight loss involves a huge amount of effort, this deserves to be recognised, acknowledged and focused on. Then this will give you the momentum to keep going and a greater reluctance to slip back.

Going public

Plans that you set for your self are more likely to be met if you also include others and tell them what you intend to do as this makes them harder to break. Likewise, successes are harder to go back on if you celebrate them publicly. So go public with all your achievements, whether it is shopping more mindfully, cooking more meals, eating at a table, being more active, walking more, doing more, going for a run, going to the gym or losing weight. And then go public with your determination to keep this going and not slip back. That way, you have made a contract not only with yourself but with everyone else as well, which makes it much harder to break.

Living the new life

Finally, the process of reinvention requires people to live the new life of the new person they have become, with being a thinner, healthier person at the core of how they see themselves. It is not good enough to think, 'I used to be overweight but now I am trying to eat well' or 'I used to do very little but now I am trying to walk more' or 'I am in a thinner phase of my life but who knows, it might all go back on'. Instead you need to redefine yourself: 'I am the kind of person who eats well', 'I walk everywhere I can and never use the lift' and 'I am a healthy person'. This can be helped by spending more time with other people who are also more healthy through joining a gym, a walking group or a running club, telling yourself that you are this new person, telling others how you now live your life and encouraging others close to you to support you in this new identity. It can also be helped by searching out role models of those who have also reinvented themselves in this way for the longer term, finding out about their stories and ignoring any stories of those who have failed as a means to offer hope that longer term change is possible.

The final step to dieting well involves paving the way forward for sustainable changes in behaviour and weight through learning to cope with failure (which is no longer seen as a failure) and the process of reinvention. This involves a number of strategies including planning, cognitive restructuring, sense making, reframing, simple repetition and modelling.

IN SUMMARY

Successful dieting involves a number of processes. Psychological theory identifies a range of behaviour change strategies. This chapter has presented a new tool kit for dieting well which is a five-step approach to pull all of this together and to use these strategies to maximise the chances of success whilst avoiding the pitfalls of failure.

10

HELPING SUCCESSFUL DIETING HAPPEN
For health professionals

Hopefully, by now it is clear that although weight loss is hard, it can happen. It should also be clear how those working in the dieting industry or as health professionals can help others more effectively. But there are also some additional issues that health professionals need to know about, which are the focus of this chapter. These include doing no harm, maximising your relationship with clients and understanding potential barriers to change.

DOING NO HARM

Dieting to lose weight can promote health and increase confidence and body esteem. It can also, however, cause harm, and it is therefore key that health professionals involved in encouraging dieting are careful of any possible negative unintended consequences. This can occur in several ways.

Does the person need to lose weight?

We live in a world where we are bombarded by images of the ideal body, and as a result, many women and men develop body dissatisfaction and therefore try to change their body size and shape through dieting. But by dieting, they may create more problems than they solve and therefore should be steered into other ways of making them feel better about themselves, including exercise, taking up a new hobby, making new friends, volunteering, singing and all the other options that are good for mood and self esteem. Dieting should only be recommended to those who are overweight or obese and need to lose weight for their health. Our relationship with food can be very fragile. For those who feel they are just a different shape than what they would like, I would suggest avoiding dieting as this might start them on a spiral of weight gain rather than weight loss.

Creating a preoccupation with food

Even with all the best behaviour change strategies, dieting always involves a degree of denial, which can ultimately lead to increased preoccupation with food and subsequent overeating. Health professionals need to be watchful of this happening in their clients and try to avoid it by minimising the notion of forbidden foods, emphasising flexible thinking rather than black and white thinking, encouraging external blame for slips, being compassionate and encouraging self compassion. If clients do start to become preoccupied with food, then this could be the time to try an alternative approach to weight loss and encourage them to become more active rather than just eating less.

Dieting as part of an eating disorder

Some people with an eating disorder are underweight and therefore easy to exclude from a dieting intervention. Others, however, may be overweight or obese but still have an eating disorder. For these, dieting can be harmful as it could exacerbate issues around food and be detrimental to their confidence and need for control. If you as a health professional start to detect a person's anxiety around food, heightened concerns about body size and shape, an overinvestment in their body shape or that they may be bingeing or purging, then the diet should be stopped and the person referred back to their GP with the suggestion that they ask for a psychological assessment.

MAXIMISING YOUR RELATIONSHIP WITH CLIENTS

Health professionals have an extremely powerful tool available to them: their relationship with the client. This relationship is often more effective at creating behaviour change than any trick of the trade that psychologists can offer and can be used in the following ways.

Being liked

At its simplest, if clients like you, they will want to please you and will be far more likely to follow your advice. So remembering your client's name, reflecting on what you have talked about in the past, smiling, listening, humour, warmth, being non-judgemental and being supportive will all help to build a good relationship. This is sometimes known as the therapeutic alliance and has been shown to improve outcomes across a wide range of very different therapeutic encounters for all sorts of conditions[95]. It would therefore also help promote dieting well.

Offering reinforcement

As a health professional, you are in the perfect position to be the reward system for anything that the client does. People are far more motivated by the carrot than the stick, so offer positive reinforcement whenever you see anything they have done that is a step in the right direction. This might be weight loss, eating more healthily or being more active. But if they haven't done this, then praise their efforts in trying to eat better, thinking about being more active or just coming back to the session. Anything good that you can praise will improve their confidence and make them want to try harder for next time.

Having follow-ups

The best predictor of weight loss maintenance by far is having longer follow-ups[79,96]. So the more you can keep people in the system for as long as possible, the better they will do. This may be because each time they come, they get reinforcement and a sense of achievement for trying. It might be because of being weighed and using this as a goal. It might be because they want to please their health professional or group leader. But it might simply be that by coming back over and over, weight loss keeps being salient, and just having it sitting there as a focus and a goal makes them more likely to keep going.

What you say

Successful weight loss involves sense making and the process of reframing across a range of domains. For example, it involves a change in the relationship with food and the associations between food, mood, social life and identity. It also requires a shift in the meanings associated with being active and doing exercise from being boring and difficult to something that is part of life. It also requires threats such as life events or symptoms to be reframed as opportunities, and the causes of being overweight need to be reframed from being biological and uncontrollable to being related to behaviour that can be changed. The relationship and the many conversations that take place between a client and a health professional are the perfect place for this sense making to start. So health professionals need to speak about healthy food as 'tasty', 'crunchy' and 'nice', not 'boring but good for you'. Exercise needs to be seen as 'fun', 'exciting', 'good for your mood' and 'a way to let off steam' rather than 'healthy' and 'necessary'. Life events should be talked about as 'Now could be time to change' or 'Use this moment to your advantage', and symptoms can be seen as 'Your body is telling you something' and 'Do something now, before it gets worse'. This doesn't need to be heavy-handed, but in the very words you choose, clients will start to take your sense making as their own, and hopefully you will hear your language coming back to you as the weeks go by.

What you do

As the health professional, you are the client's ultimate role model for what you say and what you do. And if they like you, they will want to *be* like you. Therefore the pressure is on to show them that you have a good relationship with food, eat well and enjoy being active. At times, however, they may block you by thinking, 'What do you know, you've never struggled with your weight', or if you have, 'What do you know, you're not thin either'. But this can be avoided by keeping the relationship positive and warm, building them up through reinforcement, using self affirmation or gratitude interventions and showing them images where possible rather than just using words.

UNDERSTANDING POTENTIAL BARRIERS TO CHANGE

Working with others to help them lose weight can be very difficult if they seem unable to change. But rather than becoming angry or frustrated or blaming them, it helps to understand some of the barriers to change in order to keep the relationship going and sustain a level of compassion and warmth.

The benefits of being overweight

Although from the outside, being overweight seems like a cost with all the psychological and physical consequences, many people may also find benefits in their weight. It may be a key part of their identity, a central part of their conversation, a way to avoid certain activities, a barrier against others or a way to get close to others, a way to make them unattractive to their partner or a way to make them attractive to their partner. So if a person seems resistant to change, consider how they may be benefitting from their weight, discuss this with them and look for alternative methods to achieve whatever it is that their weight is achieving for them.

The impact of partners

Although one person may want to lose weight, change their diet and be more active, this can rarely be achieved in isolation, and it is important to take into account the role of others. One key person is their partner, who may be resistant to change if they find them attractive as they are and would like their eating patterns to stay the same. When women are trying to lose weight, a male partner may be particularly resistant to change as it is still very often women in families who manage food. This can result in women changing what they eat but cooking as usual for everyone else, which is not only extra work but also isolating and can create resentment. If men are trying to lose weight but have never managed the food in the house, then this can also be problematic. It is therefore key that all family members are brought on board. This can be achieved by trying the following: thinking of weight loss as a lifestyle change for everyone rather than just a diet for some; encouraging the dieter to prepare healthier foods for everyone but just eat smaller portions themselves; explaining to the family the risks of being overweight and the benefits of weight loss; rewarding the family wherever possible for being supportive; making small changes to the content of the diet (white to brown bread, full fat milk to skimmed milk); adding foods (i.e. fruit and vegetables) rather than just taking food away (i.e. cakes and biscuits); suggesting that they have cakes and biscuits for others when out and about but get everyone to agree that they no longer will be brought into the home. Ultimately everyone in the family should want all members of the family to be well and live longer. There is much evidence that social support is key to weight loss maintenance[73,77]. Dieting therefore needs to become a shared goal so that everyone is on board.

Fear of change

Even if the status quo is unhealthy or even unpleasant, many people are still frightened of change. As a health professional, you can address this by asking clients to describe the benefits of being overweight and then to consider what their life would be like when they have lost weight. This should involve all the pros and all the cons and may well reveal feelings relating to changes in identity, humour, conversation, relationships, attractiveness, work, expectations of others and expectations of self. Strangely, even when people don't like being overweight, they don't always want to be thinner, and this needs to be discussed. It might then help to encourage them to imagine a more positive view of the future and to picture the benefits rather than the costs.

Deeply embedded habits

Weight loss and particularly weight loss maintenance are hard due to habits which may have been embedded from childhood. Trying to help someone else lose weight can be frustrating if these habits are difficult to shift. But as a health professional, it is essential that you stay compassionate, understand how difficult this is to do and just persist. Evidence shows that those who make more dieting attempts are more likely to succeed. Likewise, those health professionals who encourage more and more attempts in others are more likely to succeed as well.

IN SUMMARY

Health professionals can help others to lose weight by using the strategies described in the rest of this book and understanding the differences between failed and successful dieting. This chapter has highlighted some issues specific for health professionals. In particular, it is important to do no harm, to maximise the professional/client relationship and to use what you say, what you do and how you interact with clients as part of the process of behaviour change. If they like you and come back, they are far more likely to succeed. Finally, it is also important to recognise that losing weight and keeping it off is extremely hard, but if you stay compassionate and calm and just keep trying with your client, then they will keep trying to change and you are both much more likely to succeed.

11

HELPING OTHERS
Top tips for children

I have written a whole book on how to help children eat well without making food into a problem[19], and I remain convinced that the aim should always be to have a good relationship with food, not weight loss. However, children are becoming overweight and obese and experiencing weight-related psychological and physical problems such as lowered self esteem, anxiety, asthma and diabetes. So the aim is absolutely to develop a good relationship with food, but for overweight and obese children, the side effect of this should also be weight loss. How can this be achieved?

FIRST, DECIDE IF YOU NEED TO WORRY

I don't agree with having bathroom scales in a house with children as it can make them overly worried about their weight, and weight can become the goal rather than health. But at times it can be good to have some hard data and to know if your child is normal weight or not. So weigh your child when you can, but do it casually, without making it into a big deal. If you are staying at someone else's house who has scales, or if you are in the local chemist or at the train station, get everyone to jump on the scales 'for fun' and see what they weigh. Later, in response to someone saying something about height such as 'Mum, have I grown?', 'Tom's taller than me now' or even 'My shoes don't fit', stand them against the wall and measure their height. Then use an online child BMI checker to find out their BMI without saying anything to them. If their weight is normal, they are fine and you can ignore how much they eat. But if they are overweight, they may be developing a weight problem.

DON'T PUT THEM ON A DIET

Being a bit overweight as a child is not great. But developing a problem with eating as a child may lead to lifetime of worry and depression. If you think your child is overeating, try all the tips below to get their eating back on track, but don't put them on a diet. Going on a diet ultimately means having to deny yourself foods that you want to eat. This can make those foods seem even more tempting and in the end, when people break their diet, they eat even more than they would have done before. So limit your child's food in subtle ways by being a good role model, changing what food you buy and cook and planning meals so that children can learn to live with their hunger. But if you put them on a diet, you may well make the situation worse and food will become even more of a treat than it ever was. As time goes on, you may have set your child up for a future of struggling with one of the central parts of day to day life.

Being overweight is a product of things that are in our heads and triggers from the environment. This is the same for children, but luckily, their environment is easier to change as we control it. Below are some tips to encourage children to eat less and be more active without putting them on a diet. The last thing you want is to make food into an issue.

WHAT'S IN THEIR HEADS

From the moment we are born, the things others say to us become the scripts in our heads that carry us through life. So when we think, 'I'm good at finishing things', this was probably because our parents told us that; when we think, 'I'm lazy', that's probably our parents speaking as well. Some of these scripts relate to food and exercise, so it is important to give children positive scripts from as early as possible.

Scripts about body size

Parents need to say the right things to give their children some healthy scripts about body size. So don't say, 'We are all fat in our family. It's just the way we are', as they will believe being overweight is beyond their control and inevitable. Also don't say, 'I'm so fat. I hate it. It's so ugly' or even 'You are getting fat. You'll have no friends'. Such criticisms lead to low self esteem, self criticism and possibly comfort eating, which all make the problem worse. And don't comment on their eating, saying, 'You eat so much', 'Gosh, you can put it away', 'You have such a huge appetite' or 'You never seem to be full', as these phrases will also stick with them and they will start to see them as true and a core part of who they are. Similarly, don't praise them, saying, 'My lovely fat daughter', 'You are so fat and cuddly' or 'It's so nice having someone chubby to cuddle up to', as they will believe they need to stay overweight in order to be loved. Mostly it is best to say nothing! But if you are talking about body size, do it about someone else in a more neutral way. So when you see a celebrity of a healthy size, say, 'She looks lovely', or when a friend comes round who is normal weight, say, 'She looks really healthy'.

Scripts for being active

Parents also need to say the right things about exercise. Very often I hear 'It's boring going to the gym', 'It's too cold to go for a walk', 'Let's take the car and park in town. It's easier', 'Let's get the lift, I'm tired' and 'I've had a busy week, let's stay in this weekend and watch the TV' – all of which make exercise seem boring and as something to be avoided whenever possible. But what children need to know is that being active is a great way to manage their emotions and cheer them up when they are down, fantastic for meeting people and making friends, fun, a good method of transport, often free and a part of everyday life. So parents should use their everyday conversations to build being active in a positive way: 'Go out in the garden and let off some steam', 'Let's go for a bike ride this weekend. That will be fun', 'I'm tired. I think I'll go for a walk', 'That bike ride has made me feel so much better', 'Let's go for a walk so we can have a chat', 'I've had a busy week and really need some fresh air', 'I've met some fantastic people at netball', 'We have coffee after running which is great' and 'I have so much more energy since I've been walking to work'. That way, being active will become a positive part of life and something that is fun and a useful way to manage how we feel.

Scripts for eating well

The scripts we have for food are probably even more complicated than those we have for exercise. Watch anyone in a café with their children and you will hear, 'Ooh, that ice cream looks lovely', 'You have been so good, now eat your chocolate cake', 'If you eat your vegetables, you can have pudding', 'You have eaten all that! Well done! Now you can go in your buggy and don't have to walk', 'Guess what we have for afters – cake! Now all eat up your dinner', 'Eat your vegetables, they are healthy', 'Just eat them they are good for you' – the list goes on! The language around food builds up the scripts in our heads, and mostly they are that sweet food is a treat, that food is a useful way to manage our emotions, that healthy food is boring, that eating when you are not hungry is fine and that some foods are forbidden but exciting. So it is no surprise that as adults we turn to cake and not celery when we are down and resent trying to eat more healthily. What parents need to do is give their children more positive scripts about food in which food is nice, but not wonderful; a pleasure, but not a treat; good for you, but not boring; for hunger, but not forbidden; and sweet foods come after savoury but are not dependent on you eating the savoury foods. This is not always easy. In Table 11.1 there are some examples of what to say and not to say.

Table 11.1 Giving children positive scripts about food

Things to say	Things not to say
This shepherd's pie is great!	I know broccoli isn't very nice, but it's good for you.
This cucumber is really juicy!	
These carrots are so sweet!	Have something healthy for a change.
Well done for trying. It was quite nice really!	After tea, we can have something nice.
Well done – you did enjoy that!	
You are so good at trying new foods.	Those are Mum's biscuits, not for you. You can't have any.
You are good at knowing when to stop eating.	You do have a huge appetite!
	You are a bottomless pit!
It's good to know when you have had enough.	She does really like her pudding!
	He has a real sweet tooth!
Just eat a bit more.	Just have a small piece of cake now. Have some more tomorrow.
She's so good at eating vegetables.	
Stay at the table a bit longer.	That's enough Easter egg now. Save the rest for later.
Just a few more vegetables.	
Please don't have any more biscuits, I'm cooking dinner. You can have them afterwards.	No, you can't have pudding, not until you have eaten your meal.
	Just five more peas, please. Then you can have some ice cream.
We have a lovely melon for pudding.	Eat your vegetables, then you can have pudding.
Please wait now and have a biscuit after dinner.	You look tired. Have a piece of chocolate to give you some energy.
If you are hungry, have some fruit.	
Dinner is at 6. Just wait now.	That took me ages to cook. Please eat it all.
Here's some lovely carrot sticks to munch on before bed.	Eat that last biscuit for me, will you?

Be subtle and sometimes underhanded

At some point it is useful to have a chat about being both under- and overweight and the dangers associated with under- and overeating. But if you lecture your child over dinner or nag them in the car, they will switch off, ignore you and get cross. So be more subtle and underhanded and seize the moment in a more casual way. When you see someone on the TV who is too skinny, for example, say, 'They look dreadful. They can't be well', or when you see a mannequin in a shop window that looks very thin, say, 'No one should look like that. They would be nearly dead', or when a celebrity is being celebrated for losing vast amounts of weight, say, 'They need to be careful or they will make themselves ill'. Similarly, when you see someone on the TV who is overweight, say, 'That can't be healthy, being that size', or when a celebrity is shown having gained a huge amount of weight, say, 'Did you know that being overweight can shorten your life?'. But don't focus on the hugely obese people featured in all the programmes designed to shock as no one relates to these images and they can make people feel 'Well, I'm OK as I'm not as big as them'. This more casual, underhanded and even manipulative way of talking about size should help your children get the right scripts in their head without making food or body size into an issue.

Therefore, if parents use the right words about body size, being active and eating behaviour, children should develop healthier scripts in their head for a healthier future.

TRIGGERS IN THE ENVIRONMENT

Our body weight is also a response to triggers in our environment. When considering the weight of children, this is much easier than for adults as we mostly control their environment. In fact, often we *are* their environment.

Be a good role model for being more active

There is a well-known parenting phrase: 'If you want the people around you to change, then first change yourself'. So if your child is becoming overweight, the simplest solution is to get them to be more active, which means you have to be more active as well. This can be achieved by going for walks or family bike rides at weekends rather than watching a film, having more active holidays, showing them that you like being active by being more active and letting them see you being more active, taking up swimming or a sport, talking positively about the sport you do and taking them to the local park. It can also be achieved by simply making it easier for them to be active by buying them a ball and a skipping rope, throwing them out in the garden or street to play and encouraging them to join clubs at school. Children want to be like their parents, and if you are active, then they will want to be as well.

Be a good role model for eating

You are your child's key role model for most of their childhood, so also be a good role model for eating. This means eating well and letting them see you eating well. So eat more fruits and vegetables, eat meals and don't snack, don't skip meals, eat at a table, eat when you are hungry, don't eat to manage your emotions and have seconds if you are hungry but not if you just feel like it.

Be a good role model for body size

Also be a good role model for body size. We live in a world where people are getting fatter and being overweight has become the norm. If you are overweight, don't let your child think that this is normal, and don't encourage them to think that being overweight runs in your family and that there's nothing you can do about it. Don't moan to your child about your weight, but don't celebrate it either. Similarly, if your child is overweight, don't criticise them for it but also don't make it something to be proud of.

Change their environment

Until your child reaches the age of about 12, you are completely in charge of what they eat as you shop; you drive the car, have the money and do the cooking. Even after this age, most of what they eat is still up to you. So the best way to encourage them to eat less is to change their environment by only buying healthy foods and bringing them into the house. Don't buy fizzy drinks, crisps or biscuits if you don't want your children to eat them, and cook healthy meals without puddings. Throw grapes into the back of the car rather than crisps and give children frozen peas in front of the TV rather than sweets, and they will eat them mindlessly without realising it.

Use social pressure

Children want to be like their parents and will eventually eat what you eat. But even more powerful is the desire to be like their friends. So have children back for tea, and use this as a chance to introduce healthier foods to your child. Use social pressure to your advantage. Rather than playing safe with familiar foods cooked in familiar ways, when the pattern of your meal is changed by having someone new there, change the pattern of what you eat and get your child to try and eat foods just because their friends are doing the same.

Portion control

Strangely enough, a large plate half empty feels as if it is less than a small plate full of food! So if you feel your child is overeating and you want to limit how much they eat, make sure that you have reasonably sized plates. And all have the same plates! That way you all will be able to eat a decent-sized meal and be able to empty your plate without feeling deprived.

Plan meals

Children get hungry and will graze on whatever is available. But if there is a set time for meals when they know that they will reliably be fed, living with the hunger and waiting for the next meal becomes easier. So decide to eat at a set time whenever possible, tell your children when and what you are having for tea and ask them to wait, saying, 'It is much nicer to be hungry at tea time. You'll enjoy it more'.

Cook filling meals

If your child is hungry, they will eat in between meals. They will then eat less at meal times, be hungry shortly afterwards and eat in between meals. It is a vicious circle. So cook meals that are substantial and filling. Make sure there are plenty of carbohydrates (brown pasta, rice or bread) to fill them up and plenty of vegetables and protein. Don't cook foods that are high in fat as these may fill them up in the short term but this won't last. And avoid sugary foods as this will give them an immediate sugar high and a sense of fullness which will quickly drop right down, making them want more sugar to get the high back again.

Make small changes

The easiest way to change a habit is to do it through substitution and changes so small that you can trick your mind or the mind of others into thinking that everything is the same as it always has been. Large changes involving herbal concoctions, artichokes, fennel, lentils, seeds and nuts won't last more than a few days, if at all. But small changes are much more likely to be sustained into the longer term. So drink skimmed milk rather than whole milk and squash rather than fizzy drinks. Eat brown pasta, bread and rice rather than white and add hidden vegetables into familiar food rather than confronting your children with all new vegetables in one go. Then cook them their familiar pasta, with brown pasta rather than white, and add a new vegetable on the side and see what happens.

Eat breakfast

Breakfast is such an important meal as it kick-starts the metabolism, gets us out of the hibernation state we have been in overnight and sets us up for the day. If we miss breakfast, we stay sluggish and can't concentrate until lunchtime. So set out breakfast every morning, sit down with the children and make breakfast a normal part of the daily routine. And also get them to drink something!

Eat as a family

Eating as a family is the easiest way to set up what is healthy and that healthy is normal. So eat as a family as often as you can, and then you can be a good role model, say the right things, serve out the right food in the right portion sizes and help to make eating a normal and stress-free part of the family day.

Get a fruit bowl

Sometimes children get so hungry they can't last between meals, and the best snack available is fruit. So buy a fruit bowl, fill it with fruit and place it in a central place so they can help themselves whenever they walk by. This way they won't need unhealthy snacks but will still be hungry enough when the meal is ready.

IN SUMMARY

If you think your child is overweight, first (casually) find out their BMI and decide whether or not you really need to worry. If they are overweight, don't put them on a diet but do try to change what's in their heads as well as changing their environment. This involves offering up positive scripts about body size, food and being active as well as being a good role model for exercise and eating. It also involves managing their environment without them realising it, planning meals so that they know when food is coming and serving up filling meals so they don't snack. But do all this in an indirect, non-confrontational way as the last thing you want to do is to make food into an issue and set children off into a future of eating problems.

12

SOME CONCLUDING THOUGHTS

Nearly 30 years ago, I published *Fat Chance: The Myth of Dieting Explained* and believed that dieting did more harm than good. Since that time, there has been a massive increase in the problem of overweight and obesity in both adults and children, and I have seen the numerous psychological and physical problems caused by excessive weight gain. I have also, however, continued to see how difficult dieting is and how often dieting fails, sometimes causing more problems than it solves. But at times I have also seen examples of successful dieting, and I have gradually begun to believe that there must be a way to diet that could work not only immediately but also in the longer term. This book is the product of that very gradual process.

I still don't think that dieting is easy. Nor do I think that one approach will work for everyone. But what I do now believe is that we can learn from the evidence base for failed and successful dieting, put this together with all the psychological tricks of the trade we have for changing behaviour and work out a way to diet well. And that is what this book has tried to do.

SO MY TAKE-HOME MESSAGE IS THIS

We gain weight because we eat more than we need and do less than we should to burn off the food we eat. In turn, we overeat and are under active because of what's in our heads and the triggers in our environment. Any attempt at dieting therefore has to change what's in our heads as well as help us to manage the triggers in our environment. This is not an easy task! But going through the literature on successful and failed dieting and having an understanding of a range of behaviour change strategies indicates that a five-step approach to dieting well should help. This involves the following:

Step 1. Finding the trigger to change and reframing any kind of threat as an opportunity, then using this as the chance to change.

Step 2. Changing what's in our heads so that we believe that things can change, create a shift in the cost-benefit analysis of eating and exercise and focus on any investment made so far.

Step 3. Creating a new behaviour regimen, which involves addressing not only what you eat but where, when and why you eat.

Step 4. Managing the environment, mostly through planning and a good deal of avoidance.

Step 5. Paving the way forward through being kind to yourself, repetition and ultimately a process of reinvention.

The world is increasingly designed to make it easy to gain weight and hard to stay thin. At times the world of dieting has done more harm than good. I hope that the contents of this book help to find a pathway between these two positions and can offer a more balanced and informed way ahead.

FURTHER READING

Branch, R., and Wilson, R. (2002). *Cognitive behavioural therapy for dummies.* 2nd edition. Chichester: Wiley.

Grogan, S. (2016). *Body image: Understanding body dissatisfaction in men, women and children.* 3rd edition. London: Routledge.

Ogden, J. (1992). *Fat chance! The myth of dieting explained.* London: Routledge.

Ogden, J. (2003). *The psychology of eating: From healthy to disordered behaviour.* 2nd edition. New York and London: Blackwell.

Ogden, J. (2014). *The good parenting food guide: Managing what children eat without making food a problem.* London: Wiley.

Santos, I., Sniehotta, F.F., Marques, M.M., Carraça, E.V., and Teixeira, P.J. (2017). Prevalence of personal weight control attempts in adults: A systematic review and meta-analysis. *Obesity Reviews,* 18(1), 32–50.

Gilbert, P. (2014). The origins and nature of compassion focused therapy. *British Journal of Clinical Psychology,* March, 53(1), 6–41.

Rinzler, C.A. (2016). *Nutrition for dummies.* 6th edition. Chichester: Wiley.

REFERENCES

1 Mazel, J. (1981). *The Beverly Hills diet.* New York: MacMillan.

2 Twigg, S. (1997). *The Kensington diet.* London: Bantam Books.

3 Conley, R. (1989). *Rosemary Conley's Complete Hip and Thigh Diet.* London: Arrow Books.

4 Levine, M.J. (1997). *I wish I were thin I wish I were fat.* New York: Fireside.

5 Conley, R. (1996). *Complete flat stomach plan.* London: Arrow Books.

6 Coleman, V. (1990). *Eat green – lose weight.* London: Angus and Robertson.

7 De Vries, J. (1989). *Realistic weight control.* Edinburgh: Mainstream.

8 Lazarides, L. (1999). *The Waterfall Diet.* London: BCA.

9 Katahn, M. (1982). *The 200 calorie solution: How to stop dieting forever.* London: Arlington Books.

10 Smith, G. (1993). *Fibrenetics.* London: Fourth Estate.

11 World Health Organisation. (2016). *Obesity and overweight.* www.who.int/mediacentre/factsheets/fs311/en/ retrieved 16/4/2017

12 Pereira-Miranda, E., Costa, P.R., Queiroz, V.A., Pereira-Santos, M., and Santana, M.L. (2017). Overweight and obesity associated with higher depression prevalence in adults: A systematic review and meta-analysis. *Journal of American College of Nutrition,* April, 10, 1–11.

13 Romero-Corral, A.R., Montori, V.M., Somers, V.K., Korinek, J., Thomas, R.J., Allison, T.G., . . . Jimenez, F.L. (2006). Association of body weight with total mortality and with cardiovascular events in coronary heart disease: A systematic review of cohort studies. *Lancet,* 368, 666–678.

14 Kopelman, P. (1999). Aetiology of obesity II: Genetics, in *Obesity: The Report of the British Nutrition Foundation Task Force*, pp. 39–44. Oxford: Blackwell Science.

15 Misra, A., and Ganda, O.P. (2007). Migration and its impact on adiposity and type 2 diabetes. *Nutrition*, September, 23(9), 696–708.

16 Christakis, N.A., and Fowler, J.H. (2007). The spread of obesity in a large social network over 32 years. *New England Journal of Medicine*, July 26, 357(4), 370–379.

17 Hill, J.O., and Peters, J.C. (1998). Environmental contributions to the obesity epidemic. *Science*, 280(5368), 1371–1374.

18 Birch, L.L. (1999). Development of food preferences. *Annual Review of Nutrition*, 19, 41–62.

19 Ogden, J. (2014). *The good parenting food guide: Managing what children eat without making food a problem.* London: Wiley.

20 Koenders, P.G., and van Strien, T. (2011). Emotional eating, rather than lifestyle behavior, drives weight gain in a prospective study in 1562 employees. *Journal of Occupational and Environmental Medicine*, 53, 1287–1293.

21 Konttinen, H., Silventoinen, K., Sarlio-Lähteenkorva, S., Männistö, S., and Haukkala, A. (2010). Emotional eating and physical activity self-efficacy as pathways in the association between depressive symptoms and adiposity indicators. *American Journal of Clinical Nutrition*, 92, 1031–1039.

22 Polivy, J., and Herman, C.P. (1985). Dieting and binging: A causal analysis. *American Psychology*, February, 40(2), 193–201.

23 Hall, P.A., and Fong, G.T. (2007). Temporal self-regulation theory: A model for individual health behaviour. *Health Psychology Review*, 1(1), 6–52.

24 Ogden, J., Liakopoloulou, E., Antilliou, G., and Gough, G. (2012). The meaning of food (MOF): The development of a new measurement tool. *European Eating Disorders Review*, 20, 423–426.

25 Wansink, B. (2009). *Mindless eating: Why we eat more than we think.* 2nd edition. London: Hay House.

26 Ogden, J., Coop, N., Cousins, C., Crump, R., Field, L., Hughes, S., and Woodger, N. (2013). Distraction, the desire to eat and food intake: Towards an expanded model of mindless eating. *Appetite*, 62, 119–126.

27 Bellissimo, N., Pencharz, P.B., Thomas, S.G., and Anderson, G.H. (2007). Effect of television viewing at mealtime on food intake after a glucose preload in boys. *Pediatric Research*, 61(6), 745–749.

28 Higgs, S., and Woodward, M. (2009). Television watching during lunch increases afternoon snack intake of young women. *Appetite*, 52(1), 39–43.

29 Bolton-Smith, C., and Woodward, M. (1994). Dietary composition and fat to sugar ratios in relation to obesity. *International Journal of Obesity*, 18, 820–828.

30 Blundell, J.E., and Macdiarmid, J. (1997). Fat as a risk factor for over consumption: Satiation, satiety and patterns of eating. *Journal of the American Dietetic Association*, 97, 563–569.

31 Alsharairi, N.A., and Somerset, S.M. (2016). Skipping breakfast in early childhood and its associations with maternal and child BMI: A study of 2–5-year-old Australian children. *European Journal of Clinical Nutrition*, 70(4), 450–455.

32 Ogden, J., Oikonoumou, E., and Alemany, G. (2015). Distraction, restrained eating and disinhibition: An experimental study of food intake and the impact of 'eating on the go.' *International Journal of Health Psychology*, 22, 39–50. DOI:10.1177/1359105315595119

33 Laessle, R.G., Lehrke, S., and Dückers, S. (2007). Laboratory eating behavior in obesity. *Appetite*, 49, 399–404.

34 Shenassa, E.D., Frye, M., Braubach, M., and Daskalakis, C. (2008). Routine stair climbing in place of residence and Body Mass Index: A Pan-European population based study. *International Journal of Obesity*, 32(3), 490–494.

35 Dishman, R.K., Sallis, J.F., and Orenstein, D.M. (1985). The determinants of physical activity and exercise. *Public Health Reports*, 100, 158–172.

36 Cooney, G.M., Dwan, K., Greig, C.A., Lawlor, D.A., Rimer, J., Waugh, F.R., McMurdo, M., and Mead, G.E. (2013). Exercise for depression. *Cochrane Database of Systematic Reviews*, 9. DOI:10.1002/14651858.CD004366.pub6

37 Santos, I., Sniehotta, F.F., Marques, M.M., Carraça, E.V., and Teixeira, P.J. (2017). Prevalence of personal weight control attempts in adults: A systematic review and meta-analysis. *Obesity Reviews*, 18(1), 32–50.

38 Hirsch, J. (1998). Magic bullet for obesity. *British Medical Journal*, 317, 1136–1138.

39 Ogden, J., and Sidhu, S. (2006). Adherence, behaviour change and visualisation: A qualitative study of patient's experiences of obesity medication. *The Journal of Psychosomatic Research*, 61, 545–552.

40 Hollywood, A., and Ogden, J. (2010). Taking Orlistat: Predicting weight loss over 6 months. *Journal of Obesity*, 1–7; 806896 Open Access.

41 Picot, J., Jones, J., Colquitt, J.L., Gospodarevskaya, E., Loveman, E., and Baxter, L. (2009). The clinical effectiveness and cost-effectiveness of bariatric (weight loss) surgery for obesity: A systematic review and economic evaluation. *Health Technology Assessment*, 13, 41.

42 Sjostrom, L., Nabro, K., and Sjostrom, C.D. (2007). Effects of bariatric surgery on mortality in Swedish obese subjects. *The New England Journal of Medicine*, 357(8), 741–752.

43 Magro, D.O., Geloneze, B., Delfini, R., Paraja, B.C., Callejas, F., and Paraja, J.C. (2008). Long-term weight regain after gastric bypass: A 5-year prospective study. *Obesity Surgery*, 18(6), 648–651.

44 Ogden, J., Clementi, C., and Aylwin, S. (2006). Having obesity surgery: A qualitative study and the paradox of control. *Psychology and Health*, 21, 273–293.

45 Grogan, S. (2016). *Body image: Understanding body dissatisfaction in men, women and children*. 3rd edition. London: Routledge.

46 Tiggemann, M. (2006). The role of media exposure in adolescent girl's body dissatisfaction and drive for thinness: Prospective results. *Journal of Social and Clinical Psychology*, 25(5), 523–541.

47 Ogden, J., and Mundray, K. (1996). The effect of the media on body satisfaction: The role of gender and size. *European Eating Disorders Review*, 4, 171–182.

48 Ogden, J., and Steward, J. (2000). The role of the mother daughter relationship in explaining weight concern. *International Journal of Eating Disorders*, 28, 78–83.

49 Treasure, J., van Furth, E., and Schmidt, U. (Eds.). (2003). *Handbook of eating disorders*. 2nd edition. London: Wiley.

50 Polivy, J., and Heatherton, T. (2015). *Spiral model of dieting and disordered eating: Encyclopaedia of feeding and eating disorders*. New York: Springer.

51 Hartmann-Boyce, J., Johns, D.J., Jebb, S.A., Summerbell, C., and Aveyard, P. (2014). Behavioural weight management review group: Behavioural weight management programmes for adults assessed by trials conducted in everyday contexts: Systematic review and meta-analysis. *Obesity Reviews*, November, 15(11), 920–932.

52 Dombrowski, S.U., Knittle, K., Avenell, A., Araújo-Soares, V., and Sniehotta, F.F. (2014). Long term maintenance of weight loss with non-surgical interventions in obese adults: Systematic review and meta-analyses of randomised controlled trials. *BMJ*, May 14, 348.

53 Ahern, A.L., Olson, A.D., Aston, L.M., and Jebb, S.A. (2011). Weight Watchers on prescription: An observational study of weight change among adults referred to Weight Watchers by the NHS. *BMC Public Health*, June 6, 11, 434.

54 Colquitt, J.L., Pickett, K., Loveman, E., and Frampton, G.K. (2014). Surgery for weight loss in adults. *Cochrane Database of Systematic Reviews*, August 8. DOI: 10.1002/14651858.CD003641.pub4

55 Aucott, L.S. (2008). Influences of weight loss on long-term diabetes outcomes. *Proceedings of Nutrition Society*, February, 67(1), 54–59.

56 Blackburn, G. (1995). Effect of degree of weight loss on health benefits. *Obesity Reviews*, September, 3(Supplement 2), 211s-216s.

57 Lissner, L., Odell, P.M., D'Agostino, R.B., Stokes, J., Kreger, B.E., Belanger, A.J., and Brownell, K.D. (1991). Variability of body weight and health outcomes in the Framingham population. *New England Journal of Medicine*, 324, 1839–1844.

58 Wegner, D.M. (1994). Ironic processes of mental control. *Psychological Review*, 101, 34–52.

59 Polivy, J., and Herman, C.P. (1999). Distress and eating: Why do dieters overeat? *International Journal of Eating Disorders*, 26, 153–164.

60 Orbell, S., and Verplanken, B. (2015). The strength of habit. *Health Psychology Review*, 9(3), 311–317.

61 Lally, P., and Gardner, B. (2013). Promoting habit formation. *Health Psychology Review*, (Supplement 1), S137–S158.

62 Ogden, J., and Hills, L. (2008). Understanding sustained changes in behaviour: The role of life events and the process of reinvention. *Health: An International Journal*, 12, 419–437.

63 Epiphaniou, E., and Ogden, J. (2010). Successful weight loss maintenance: From a restricted to liberated self. *International Journal of Health Psychology*, 15, 887–896.

64 Ogden, J., Clementi, C., and Aylwin, S. (2006). Having obesity surgery: A qualitative study and the paradox of control. *Psychology and Health*, 21, 273–293.

65 Wood, K., and Ogden, J. (in press). Obesity Patients' long-term experiences following obesity surgery with a focus on eating behaviour: A qualitative study. *Journal of Health Psychology*.

66 Greaves, C., Poltawski, L., Garside, R., and Briscoe, S. (2017). Understanding the challenge of weight loss maintenance: A systematic review and synthesis of qualitative research on weight loss maintenance. *Health Psychology Review*, April 7, 1–19.

67 Thomas, J.G., Bond, D.S., Phelan, S., Hill, J.O., and Wing, R.R. (2014). Weight-loss maintenance for 10 years in the National Weight Control Registry. *American Journal of Preventive Medicine*, January, 46(1), 17–23.

68 Bachman, J.L., Phelan, S., Wing, R.R., and Raynor, H.A. (2011). Eating frequency is higher in weight loss maintainers and normal-weight individuals than in overweight individuals. *Journal of American Dietetics Association*, November, 111(11), 1730–1734.

69 Bond, D.S., Phelan, S., Leahey, T.M., Hill, J.O., and Wing, R.R. (2009). Weight-loss maintenance in successful weight losers: Surgical vs non-surgical methods. *International Journal of Obesity* (London), January, 33(1), 173–180.

70 Wing, R.R., Papandonatos, G., Fava, J.L., Gorin, A.A., Phelan, S., McCaffery, J., and Tate, D.F. (2008). Maintaining large weight losses: The role of behavioral and psychological factors. *Journal of Consulting and Clinical Psychology*, December, 76(6), 1015–1021.

71 Butryn, M.L., Phelan, S., Hill, J.O., and Wing, R.R. (2007). Consistent self-monitoring of weight: A key component of successful weight loss maintenance. *Obesity* (Silver Spring), December, 15(12), 3091–3096.

72 Phelan, S., and Wing, R.R. (2005). Prevalence of successful weight loss. *Archives of Internal Medicine*, November 14, 165(20), 2430.

73 Wing, R.R., and Phelan, S. (2005). Long-term weight loss maintenance. *American Journal of Clinical Nutrition*, July, 82 (Supplement 1), 222S–225S. Review. PubMed PMID: 16002825.

74 Ogden, J. (2000). The correlates of long terms weight loss: A group comparison study of obesity. *International Journal of Obesity*, 24, 1018–1025.

75 Elfhag, K., and Rössner, S. (2005). Who succeeds in maintaining weight loss? A conceptual review of factors associated with weight loss maintenance and weight regain. *Obesity Reviews*, February, 6(1), 67–85.

76 Epiphaniou, E., and Ogden, J. (2010). Evaluating the role of triggers and sustaining conditions in weight loss maintenance. *Journal of Obesity*, 1–7; 8594143 Open Access.

77 Stubbs, J., Whybrow, S., Teixeira, P., Blundell, J., Lawton, C., Westenhoefer, J., . . . Raats, M. (2011). Problems in identifying predictors and correlates of weight loss and maintenance: Implications for weight control therapies based on behaviour change. *Obesity Reviews*, September, 12(9), 688–708.

78 Teixeira, P.J., Carraça, E.V., Marques, M.M., Rutter, H., Oppert, J.M., De Bourdeaudhuij, I., . . . Brug, J. (2015). Successful behavior change in obesity

interventions in adults: A systematic review of self-regulation mediators. *BMC Medicine*, April 16, 13, 84.

79 Hartmann-Boyce, J., Johns, D.J., Jebb, S.A., and Aveyard, P. (2014). Behavioural weight management review group: Effect of behavioural techniques and delivery mode on effectiveness of weight management: Systematic review, meta-analysis and meta-regression. *Obesity Reviews*, July, 15(7), 598–609.

80 NHS Choices. *Cognitive behavioural therapy*. www.nhs.uk/Conditions/Cognitive-behavioural-therapy/Pages/Introduction.aspx retrieved 17/4/2017

81 Marlatt, G.A., and Gordon, J.R. (Ed.). (1985). *Relapse prevention: Maintenance strategies in the treatment of addictive behaviors*. New York: Guilford Press.

82 Leventhal, H., Benyamini, Y., Brownlee, S., Diefenbach, M., Leventhal, EA., Patrick-Miller, L., and Robitaille, C. (1997). Illness representations: Theoretical foundations, in K.J. Petrie and J.A. Weinman (eds.), *Perceptions of Health and Illness*, pp. 1–18. Amsterdam: Harwood.

83 Carver, C.S., and Scheier, M.F. (1999). Stress, coping, and self-regulatory processes, in L.A. Pervin and J.P. Oliver (eds.), *Handbook of Personality Theory and Research*, pp. 553–575. New York: Guildford Press.

84 Hagger, M. S., Luszczynska, A., de Wit, J., Benyamini, Y., Burkert, S., Chamberland, P.-E., . . . Gollwitzer, P. M. (2016). Implementation intention and planning interventions in health psychology: Recommendations from the Synergy expert group for research and practice. *Psychology & Health*, 31(7), 814–839.

85 DiClemente, C.C., and Prochaska, J.O. (1985). Processes and stages of change: Coping and competence in smoking behavior change, in F. Shiffman and T.A. Wills (eds.), *Coping and Substance Abuse*, pp. 319–343. New York: Academic Press.

86 Miller, W., and Rollnick, S. (2002). *Motivational interviewing: Preparing people to change addictive behaviour*. New York: Guilford Press.

87 Festinger, L. (1957). *A theory of cognitive dissonance*. Evanston, IL: Row, Peterson.

88 Ruiter, R.A.C., Abraham, C., and Kok, G. (2001). Scary warnings and rational precautions: A review of the psychology of fear appeals. *Psychology and Health*, 16(6), 613–630.

89 Cameron, L.D. (2009). Can our health behaviour models handle imagery-based processes and communications? Keynote Article 1. *The European Health Psychologist*, 11, 56–58.

90 Harris, P.R., and Upton, T. (2009). The impact of self-affirmation on health cognition, health behaviour and other health-related responses: A narrative review. *Social and Personality Psychology Compass*, 3(6), 962–978.

91 Husted, M., and Ogden, J. (2014). Impact of an investment based intervention on weight-loss and hedonic thoughts about food post-obesity surgery. *Journal of Obesity.* 1–8 DOI:10.1155/2014/810374

92 Rogers, P.J. (2016). Breakfast: How important is it really? *Public Health Nutrition,* June, 19(9), 1718–1719.

93 Ogden, J., Wood, C., Payne, E., Fouracre, H., and Lammyman, F. (in press). 'Snack' versus 'meal': the impact of label and place on food intake. *Appetite.*

94 Gilbert, P. (2014). The origins and nature of compassion focused therapy. *British Journal of Clinical Psychology,* March, 53(1), 6–41.

95 Krupnick, J.L., Sotsky, S.M., Simmens, S., Moyer, J., Elkin, I., Watkins, J., and Pilkonis, P.A. (1996). The role of the therapeutic alliance in psychotherapy and pharmacotherapy outcome: Findings in the national institute of mental health treatment of depression collaborative research program. *Journal of Consulting and Clinical Psychology,* 64(3), 532–539.

96 Johns, D.J., Hartmann-Boyce, J., Jebb, S.A., and Aveyard, P. (2014). Behavioural weight management review group: Diet or exercise interventions vs combined behavioural weight management programs: A systematic review and meta-analysis of direct comparisons. *Journal of Academy of Nutrition and Dietetics,* October, 114(10), 1557–1568.

Printed in the United States
by Baker & Taylor Publisher Services